An Irish Farmhouse Cookbook

Mary Kinsella

Appletree Press

First printed and published in 1983 by
The Appletree Press Ltd
7 James Street South
Belfast BT2 8DL

ISBN 0 86281 100 9

Copyright © Mary Kinsella, 1983

Cover photograph: near Kylemore, Co. Galway
John Murphy

10   9   8   7   6

Contents

Galloping Horseshoe — Chicken Roast — Christmas Turkey — Turkey Pie —
Golden Goose — Creamy Pheasant — Rabbit Stew

VEGETABLES 102

Colcannon — Champ — Boxty — Potato Cakes — Whipped Potatoes — Cottage
Potatoes — Roast Potatoes — Savoury Baked Potatoes — Hot Potato Salad — Best
Chips — Old Fashioned Chips — Potato and Onion Pie — Vegetables in a Shell —
Tomatoes in Sour Cream — Dressed Mushrooms — Stuffed Cabbage Rolls — Cauli-
flower in all its Glory — Fried Leeks and Bacon — Stuffed Vegetable Marrow —
Buttered Celery — Vegetable Hotpot — Buttered Carrots — Carrot and Parsnip
Mash — Creamy Swedes — Crowned Beetroot

SAUCES 118

White Sauce — Pouring Sauce — Stewing Sauce — Coating Sauce — Panard Sauce —
Parsley Sauce — Onion Sauce — Caper Sauce — Cheese Sauce — Mustard Sauce —
Bechamel Sauce — Bread Sauce — Horseradish Sauce — Hollandaise Sauce —
Tomato Sauce — Mint Sauce — Curry Sauce — Brown Sauce — Brown Gravy —
Orange Sauce — Apple Sauce — Sour Cream Sauce — Thick Mayonnaise — Egg
Dressing — Salad Dressing — Whiskey Sauce — Custard Sauce — Almond Cream
Sauce — Rich Pastry Cream — Chocolate Sauce — Jam Sauce

SALADS 127

Green Salad — Asparagus Salad — Egg and Bean Salad — Fish Salad — Chicken
Salad — Apple and Sausage Salad — Orange and Liver Salad — Ham and Pineapple
Salad — Tongue Salad — Stuffed Meat Salad — Coleslaw

PASTRY 133

Suggestions on Pastry Making — Shortcrust Pastry — Fleur Pastry — Biscuit Pastry —
Rough Puff Pastry — Flaky Pastry — Puff Pastry — Choux Pastry

TEA AND SUPPER CAKES 138

Hints on Baking — Preparation of Cake Tins — What Went Wrong? Baking Watch-
points — Barm Brack — Gingerbread — Almond Rings — Rock Buns — Doughnuts —
Porter Cake — Four-Egg Sponge — Jam Sponge Roll — Sponge Flan Shell — Coffee
Cake — Basic Cake — Mother's Cake — Seed Cake — Chapel Window — Orange
Cake — Cherry Cake — Chocolate Marble Cake — Walnut Layer Cake — Mincemeat
Cheesecake — Light Fruitcake — Apple Fruitcake — Christmas Cake Kinsella —
Rich Fruitcake — Poitín Cake — Almond Paste — Royal Icing

DESSERTS 162

Everyday Sweet — Shortbread Pie — Date and Cherry Pudding — Heart of Ireland —
Gooseberry and Custard Tart — Crowned Rhubarb — Flann Eireann — Mincemeat
Flan — Sunshine Treat — Fruit Shells — Strawberry Basket — Sherry Trifle — Log of
Almond — Cherry Chocolate — Sponge Cheesecake — Black Forest — Sweet
Almond Pancakes — Honey Pie — Mist Biscuit — Orchard Pride — Chocolate Pears
— Apple Float — Strawberry Cream — Gaelige Ice Cream

GLOSSARY 181

Introduction

There is an old saying in Ireland that you can take the man away from the bog but you can't take the bog away from the man. Most Irish men—and women—have some connection with country life, and happy memories of time spent on the farm.

Because ours is so much an agricultural country, we Irish have a great deal to be thankful for. We have an abundance of fresh meat, fresh dairy products, fresh vegetables and fruit. We live on an island surrounded by water, and our seas, rivers and streams abound in fish.

We are especially fortunate in being born and brought up on a farm—a progressive mixed farm that gave us nearly all the meat we wanted. We rarely bought anything from the butcher. We always had hens, chickens, geese, ducks and turkeys in plenty. We had eggs from our own fowl houses. We had butter from our own dairy, and I often took my turn at that old churn.

My mother still makes her own country butter. It costs more these days, but she does it for the flavour. It is second nature to us, when we're at home, to go over to the dairy, separate the milk from the cream, churn the cream, make the butter. We help gather eggs from the fowl house and in the summer we go out and pick the fresh berries—the strawberries, raspberries, gooseberries, blackberries, blackcurrants—just as we did when we were children and later when home on holidays from boarding school. In years gone by, the fruit was preserved in syrups or in the jam we made at home; these days we can keep it in the big freezer all year round in its original form. In autumn we still climb trees as we used to, to collect apples, pears and plums. When we were younger we'd climb the top of a favourite tree to get the juiciest black plums for our parents.

Everyone loved mother's fruit tarts. Her pastry was unique. Mother was anxious to instil in us all—I have five older sisters—her love of cooking and her high standards. It was a family tradition, passed down to her from her mother, and from her to us. She never weighed the flour, and would often add a quantity of cream to enrich it. One day, as I watched her work that magic of hers with tarts and cakes, I suddenly realized that if I were ever going to be able to make her recipes my own, I'd have to put them on paper myself. So the next time she was baking I stopped her at every stage, weighed each ingredient she was using, and wrote it all down.

My mother was the one who inspired me with a great desire to make a life's work of carrying on the tradition. and it was she who most encouraged me when I decided to make a career as a cook and a teacher of cooking, to spend all my time learning more and more about cookery and passing on what I learned to others. Through the years I've worked as a teacher and lecturer with hundreds of people. I've tried very hard to understand their cooking problems. In assembling and writing this book I've done my utmost to make everything as clear and simple and natural as possible.

My hope is that readers who use my recipes will find cooking a great pleasure, as I do. My special hope is that they will find satisfaction and great success

Mary Kinsella
Tomadilly
Enniscorthy
Co. Wexford
Ireland

Cooking Methods

SIMMERING

Food cooked steadily in liquid over a heat so gentle that a bubble will occasionally appear on the surface.

POACHING

Cooking food in a small amount of quietly simmering liquid.

FRYING

There are three methods:

Dry Frying: When food containing plenty of natural fat is cooked on a hot pan without the addition of fat (bacon for example).

Shallow Frying: When food is cooked in small amounts of butter or oil or other fat.

Deep Frying: When food is cooked in a deep saucepan with enough fat to completely cover up the food. Usually the fat will fill about half the pot. The food is put in a wire basket and then lowered into the hot fat. Deep frying is a very good method of preparing leftover food (for instance pre-cooked meat, fish and potatoes).

Hints on Deep Frying

1. The fat must be smoking hot. The temperature may be tested by putting a one-inch cube of bread into the hot fat. After 40 to 60 seconds the bread, now golden brown, should rise to the top.
2. Coat the food with egg and breadcrumbs or with batter.
3. Put the food into a wire basket and lower the basket slowly into fat.
4. Cook the food in small quantities to prevent lowering the temperature of fat, which would spoil the food. Fat must be re-heated before any more food is put in to fry.
5. When the food is golden brown, remove from fat and immediately drain it on kitchen paper.
6. Strain fat into a clean bowl. It will keep for several months, and can be used while it lasts.

ROASTING

Cooking meat on some form of spit over direct heat; it is best done over a strong heat. The rotisserie is a modern method of roasting.

BAKING

Meat put into a roasting tin and set into the oven is really baked; it is incorrect to call it roasting. Only the best quality of meat should be used for roasting or baking.

STEWING

Long slow cooking in liquid over a gentle heat in a covered saucepan on the

7

stove top. Good for cheaper cuts of meat, mixed with potatoes and vegetables.

CASSEROLLING

Stewing done in heat-proof dish in the oven. Also called hot pot.

POT ROASTING

A misnomer (see baking) but one of the best methods of cooking tougher cuts of meat like brisket. The meat is put in a covered saucepan and cooked on the stove top or on the oven in little fat over a gentle heat, sometimes with a little liquid added.

BRAISING

Cooking, often of cheaper cuts of meat, by a combination of stewing, steaming and baking. The meat is browned in a little hot fat, then laid on a bed of prepared vegetables (with enough water or stock to cook them) in a pot or casserole dish with a tight-fitting lid. Braising may be done on the stove top or in the oven.

WEIGHTS AND MEASURES

An important point to remember with regard to solid measures. Irish cooks are generous with their teaspoon and tablespoon measures: these are usually heaped, while the American cook levels off the quantity on the spoon with a knife. So it is important to note that where a recipe specifies a teaspoon of sugar, for example, you should use a rounded teaspoonful, i.e. as much above the spoon as in it, or **two** level teaspoonfuls.

Breakfast Dishes

TRADITIONAL IRISH BREAKFAST

For the French, breakfast might be only a glass of *jus d'orange,* a croissant and a cup of *cafe noir.* For the Irish, breakfast means a serious break in the overnight fast, and to prove their seriousness, they indulge themselves in a full meal. This typically means fruit juice followed by hot or cold cereal, and then a big grill or fry of rashers (strips of bacon), sausages and an egg or two, garnished with slices of tomato and served with toast and plenty of soda bread lashed with butter and accompanied by a pot of strong tea. Some details of the traditional breakfast:

ORANGE JUICE

Though oranges are not native to Ireland, we've become very partial to them. Fixing fresh orange juice is simple enough.

Ingredients: Serves: 1

1–2 large oranges
2 teaspoons sugar (optional)

Method

1. Cut the orange in half.
2. Using an orange squeezer, squeeze out the orange juice.
3. Strain juice into a glass.
4. Add sugar if desired.
5. Chill and serve.

PORRIDGE

Ingredients: Serves: 6

1 pint water		
pinch of salt		
2 oz oatmeal	**575 ml**	2½ cups
	100 g	¾ cup

Preparation time: 5 minutes   **Cooking time:** 10–15 minutes

Method

1. Bring the water to the boil in a saucepan.
2. Add the salt and sprinkle in the oats, stirring continually to prevent lumps from forming.
3. Boil and stir for a few minutes.

   Cover and simmer for 10–15 minutes.
4. Pour into individual bowls and serve with sugar and milk.

RASHERS, EGG, SAUSAGE AND TOMATO

Some people call them rashers, others say bacon. At home in my County Wexford we always called them back rashers. They had plenty of lean meat. When we fried eggs at home we would always prick the yolk with a fork to spread it out over the egg white. When the egg was set we would turn it over and fry the other side for an extra minute or so. Most city people fry the egg in a few tablespoonfuls of fat, taking care not to break the yolk. When the egg white is set they spoon the fat over the yolk until the yolk is firm. This makes for a richer appearance. I find myself using both methods.

Most children love sausages. When we were young my sisters and I would get up at about eight on a Sunday morning when all the other members of the family were gone to Mass. We had the house to ourselves and could prepare our breakfast our own way. One of us would go out to the dairy for the milk and butter. Another would set the table and the oldest of the three of us would put the big black heavy pan on the cooker. There was always plenty of fat in the pan. We cooked six sausages until they were golden brown all over, and served them up with plenty of fat from the pan, and with slices of mother's soda bread spread thickly with butter.

Ingredients: Serves: 1

2 slices of bacon
2 sausages
fried .egg(s)
1 tomato
finely chopped parsley (optional)

Preparation time: 5 minutes   **Cooking time:** 8–10 minutes

Method:

1. Remove rind from rashers (not a problem with US and Canadian rashers).
2. Set the rashers and sausages on a preheated grill (set at maximum).
3. Cook rashers until as crisp as desired on both sides. Cook sausages until golden brown all over.
4. Slice tomato in half; begin grilling after turning rashers onto the second side.
5. Fry the egg and set it in the centre of the plate; arrange rashers, sausages and tomato around the edge.
6. Garnish, if you like, with finely chopped parsley.

To vary: Fry the rashers and sausages. If frying, cooking will ideally be done a bit more slowly. The best way is to begin by putting the rashers or sausages onto a cold lightly greased frying pan over a gentle heat. As the fat is released from the rashers or sausages, gradually increase the heat.

Be sure to cook sausages on all sides. They should be a golden brown after 10 minutes. Turn bacon onto the other side after 4–5 minutes and cook a further 4 minutes.

FRIED EGGS

egg(s)
2 tablespoons or so of oil or bacon fat

Preparation time: 3 minutes   **Cooking time:** 4–5 minutes

Method:

1. Heat the oil or fat until blue smoke rises.
2. Drop egg(s) in, then remove from heat for a minute.
3. Return to a gentle heat, tilt the pan to one side and with a tablespoon pour the hot oil or fat over egg until yolk and white is well set.
4. Remove from pan and serve hot.

To vary: Margarine can be substituted for either of the above. Butter is a problem; it tends to burn in the hot pan. If butter is used, set heat lower and allow longer cooking time. To prevent butter burning add a little oil to the pan.

Watchpoint: You may prefer frying eggs one at a time, to get a nice even finish. Singly, eggs are more easily managed.

TRADITIONAL EGG DISHES

In the country, particularly in summertime, fresh eggs were plentiful. We always kept a few dozen hens in the fowlhouse at home; they fed on barley meal, skim milk and the scraps in the yard.

Mother kept leghorn hens, elegant-looking creatures with fine white feathers which laid lovely white eggs. But they were real devils, and nested in the most unusual places, so that during the summer months gathering eggs was particularly difficult: when laying, the hens would repair to the very top of the sheds where bales of hay and straw were stored.

During July and August we used to preserve eggs by putting them into big buckets and pouring a preserving solution over them. These were saved for making Christmas cakes and puddings served during the holiday season, when eggs tended to be more expensive.

SOFT BOILED EGGS

fresh egg(s)
pinch of salt
boiling water

Cooking time: 5 minutes

Method:

1. Bring water to a gentle boil.
2. Put egg(s) and salt into saucepan (the salt keeps eggs from breaking); cover egg(s) with

boiling water.

HARD-BOILED EGGS

1. As for soft-boiled eggs, but cook for 8 to 10 minutes.
2. Pour off boiling water; pour cold water over egg(s) to pre-

3. Simmer for 5 minutes.

vent black ring forming around the yolk.

3. Break and remove the shell.

POACHED EGG

fresh egg
1 teaspoon of vinegar or pinch of salt
boiling water

Cooking time: 3–4 minutes

Method:

1. Put egg into boiling water and count up to 20, then remove. Break the egg into a cup.
2. Lower the heat. Swirl water twice with a spoon. Drop the

egg into the centre of the water.
3. Cook for 3 or 4 minutes.
4. When egg is ready, remove from the water and slip into a bowl of cold water.

SCRAMBLED EGGS

2 eggs
1 tablespoon milk
seasoning
$1\frac{1}{2}$ tablespoons butter or margarine
finely chopped parsley (optional)

Cooking time: 1–2 minutes

Method:

1. Beat eggs, milk and seasoning together.
2. Melt half the butter in a saucepan over moderate heat. Add the seasoned eggs.
3. Stir from the beginning with a fork. When the eggs form into

large flakes, add remaining butter.
4. Cook for 1 or 2 minutes.
5. Remove from heat, garnish with chopped parsley.
6. Serve on buttered toast.

BUTTERED EGGS

Cook as for scrambled eggs, omitting milk.

BAKED EGGS(S)

egg(s)
$\frac{3}{4}$ tablespoon butter

12

Preparation time: 6–8 minutes
Oven position: centre

Cooking time: 6–8 minutes
Oven temperature:
gas 5, 190°C, 375°F

Method:

1. Put butter into a small oven-proof dish and put into the oven until the butter is melted.
2. Season eggs to taste and put them in the heated dish.
3. Put in oven for 6 to 8 minutes.

PLAIN OMELET

2 eggs
seasoning
1 tablespoon milk
$\frac{3}{4}$ tablespoon butter or margarine

Cooking time: 3–4 minutes

Method:

1. Beat eggs, seasoning and milk lightly together with a fork.
2. Heat the butter or margarine until it begins to foam.
3. Preheat serving plate.
4. Pour in the seasoned eggs, shake the pan and stir eggs slowly with the back of a fork. Rest for a few seconds to allow cooking to proceed.
5. Tilt the pan a little and begin to fold edge over so that the liquid on top will escape from the middle of the omelet and come into contact with the hot base of the pan.
6. When omelet is just set, tilt pan so that omelet rolls over on itself. Turn onto preheated plate.

SAVOURY OMELET

One evening at teatime an older sister of mine introduced the younger children in the family to savoury omelets. We had never seen mother make them so we were very excited. My sister made sure that we were seated at the table, so that the omelets could be served piping hot straight from the pan. Our eyes lit up when the first omelet arrived, beautiful and filled with chopped fresh herbs.

Ingredients:

As for plain omelet, but spoon over the filling before folding omelet in half.

Method:

1. Two ounces (50 g, $\frac{1}{2}$ cup) of any of the following: diced cooked bacon, cooked mushrooms, grated cheese, cooked vegetables.
2. Then proceed.

13

BACON AND CHEESE SLICES

Toast was a luxury in our house. We never had a modern toaster at home. We had a large cooker, though; it had four ovens with various heat settings. There were two big cooking plates, one very hot and the other the simmer plate. Both had tight lids. To make the toast we put the sliced bread between a double wire rack on the hot plate. The rack was like a tennis racket with hinges at the top. The rack was placed over the hot plate and the lid brought down, covering it for four or five minutes until the toast was nicely browned. Today grills make bacon and cheese slices easier to cook.

Ingredients: Serves: 2

4 slices bread		
1 oz butter	**25 g**	1½ tbsp.
mustard to taste		
4 slices bacon		
2 oz grated cheese	**50 g**	½ cup
chopped parsley		

Preparation time: 15 minutes   **Cooking time:** 10 minutes

Method:

1. Toast the bread until golden brown on one side; butter the other side, spread with mustard, and keep warm.
2. Stretch each slice of bacon using the back of a knife and cut in two.
3. Grill the bacon, allowing 3 minutes for each side.
4. Set the bacon on buttered toast and sprinkle with grated cheese.
5. Set under the grill until nicely browned.
6. Serve immediately, garnished with chopped parsley.

GOLDEN PLAICE

Plaice is widely used in our menus, even for breakfast, because it is available all year round and is reasonably priced. It has the virtue of its blandness; various herbs and seasonings can be added to vary the flavour.

There are several American flat white fish that can be substituted for plaice. Sole would work well in a plaice recipe, though it has more flavour and in Ireland is more expensive. Halibut or turbot would also serve, as would cod, hake, whitefish and haddock.

Ingredients: Serves: 2

4 slices bread		
1 oz butter	**25 g**	1½ tbsp.
1 oz margarine	**25 g**	1½ tbsp.

1 oz flour	**25 g**	¼ cup
½ pint milk	**275 ml**	1¼ cups
8 oz cooked flaked plaice	**200 g**	1 cup
2 oz grated cheese	**50 g**	½ cup
seasoning		

Preparation time: 15 minutes   Cooking time: 5–7 minutes

Method:

1. Toast bread on one side, butter non-toasted side.
2. Melt margarine, add flour and cook for a minute; gradually add the milk, bring to the boil and season to taste.
3. Add the fish, bring back to the boil.
4. Divide fish, spreading it evenly on slices of buttered bread.
5. Sprinkle with grated cheese and set under the grill until golden brown.
6. Serve immediately.

SAVOURY FISH CAKES

Meat was always available at home. But we relied on a good neighbour for fresh fish from the river, except on Thursday nights when we travelled to the nearest fishing village some distance from home to get fish for the main Friday meal. To stretch our supply of fish we made fish cakes.

Ingredients: Serves: 4

8 oz cooked fish		
(whiting, haddock, cod)	**200 g**	1 cup
8 oz cooked potatoes	**200 g**	1 cup
1 finely chopped onion		
1 oz melted butter or margarine	**25 g**	1½ tbsp.
seasoning		
1 oz margarine	**25 g**	1½ tbsp.
(or 2 tablespoons oil)		oil
finely chopped parsley		

Preparation time: 15 minutes   Cooking time: 10–15 minutes

Method:

1. Flake fish and mash the potatoes.
2. Combine fish, potatoes, onion, melted butter or margarine together. Season to taste.
3. Divide the mixture into eight parts, shape into circular small cakes two inches in diameter.
4. Coat with milk and breadcrumbs.
5. Melt fat in frying pan; fry fish cakes until golden brown.
6. Serve hot, garnished with chopped parsley.

15

CREAMY MUSHROOMS

Wild mushrooms were a common sight here a few years ago. Within a few hours after a hot wet August day, mushrooms would spring right up out of the ground—mushrooms with a beautiful juicy flavour that could be gathered in by the basketful. When they were washed and the skin was removed, with a knob of butter on each, they were laid out on a baking sheet, and were generously seasoned. They were lovely when eaten with fresh soda bread and butter. Cultivated mushrooms—Ireland exports tons of them—are far more readily available these days but the flavour can't be compared with that of the wild ones.

Ingredients: Serves: 2

4 slices bread		
1 oz butter	**25 g**	1½ tbsp.
1 tablespoon oil		
4 oz cleaned and sliced mushrooms	**100 g**	¾ cup
1 oz flour	**25 g**	¼ cup
½ pint milk	**275 ml**	1¼ cups
2 tomatoes		
1 tablespoon finely chopped parsley		
seasoning		

Preparation time: 15 minutes   **Cooking time:** 10 minutes

Method:

1. Toast bread on one side, spread butter on the other. Keep warm.
2. Heat oil in a saucepan, and gently fry the mushrooms.
3. Add flour and cook for a minute. Then gradually add milk and lemon juice, and bring to the boil. Add parsley and season to taste. Simmer for 3–4 minutes.
4. Cut tomatoes in half and grill.
5. Place toast on serving dish, arrange creamy mushrooms on top of toast; garnish with a grilled tomato and sprinkle with parsley. Serve hot.

WEIGHTS AND MEASURES

An important point to remember with regard to solid measures. Irish cooks are generous with their teaspoon and tablespoon measures: these are usually heaped, while the American cook levels off the quantity on the spoon with a knife. So it is important to note that where a recipe specifies a teaspoon of sugar, for example, you should use a rounded teaspoonful, i.e. as much above the spoon as in it, or **two** level teaspoonfuls.

Bread and Scones

In former years an Irish housewife made fresh soda bread every day. Some of the oats, barley and wheat harvested during August and September were stored in the loft. Grains of each kind were spread out on the loft floor, and every month bags of grains were filled and brought to the mill where they were finely ground to be used in breads—oatenmeal, wheatenmeal and bran.

HINTS FOR MAKING BREAD AND SCONES

1. When making bread with baking soda, buttermilk or sour milk should be used; when making it with baking powder, whole milk (sweet milk) must be used.
2. Brown bread can be of a light or coarse texture, the amount of wholemeal varying according to taste. A greater proportion of wholemeal to plain flour will make the bread more nutritious; it will also produce a coarser bread.
3. The addition of bran makes bread very rich and nutritious.
   dried fruit.
4. To vary scones, add a half cup or so of grated cheese or half cup or so of dried fruit.
5. Always set bread or scones out on a lightly floured baking sheet or casserole dish. And keep in mind that too much flour can spoil their taste and appearance.
6. Brushing the scones or bread with milk or egg and milk, gives them a better appearance. If egg is used in the recipe, always keep back a little, add some milk and a pinch of salt, beat together with a fork, and use this to brush the baked pieces.
7. To get a soft crust on bread put the dough in a casserole. Keep the lid on during cooking, allowing an extra five minutes cooking time.
8. Always set baked bread out on a wire rack as soon as it is baked or else stand it on end. This is to make sure that it will cool all around. If set out otherwise it will become soggy.
9. Bread or scones can be made in large quantities. When they're baked and cooled, they can be wrapped and put into the freezer.

SPEEDY BREAD

Ingredients:

1 lb flour	**500 g**	4 cups
2 teaspoons baking powder		
(or 1 lb self-raising flour)		

pinch of salt
½ pint sweet milk   **275 ml**   1¼ cups

Preparation time: 10 minutes   **Cooking time:** 40–45 minutes

Oven position: top   **Oven temperature:** gas 6, 200°C, 400°F

Method:
1. Lightly flour a baking sheet.
2. Sieve flour and salt into a bowl. Add baking powder (if used).
3. Make a well in the centre and add almost all the milk; mix to a loose dough. If necessary add more milk.
4. Turn onto a floured board and knead for five minutes until smooth.
5. Shape dough into a circular shape; make cross-cut on surface and place on floured baking sheet, put into the oven.
6. When baked, place on wire rack to cool.

SWEET BREAD

Method:
1. Add to above ingredients 3 tablespoons butter or margarine, 2 or 3 tablespoons sugar, 1 egg yolk.
2. Cut and rub butter or margarine into the flour.
3. Add sugar and egg yolk. Add milk and mix to a loose dough.

SODA BREAD

Fresh country buttermilk, which makes beautiful soda bread, is hard to come by today; most farmers send their milk direct to the creamery. But my mother still churns the cream twice a week, and from the buttermilk makes at least three large loaves of bread every day. She makes brown soda during the week and white soda bread for Sunday. The buttermilk ordinarily used in making soda bread gave the crust a rich golden brown colour. But all the ingredients in soda bread were nutritious—and fresh.

Our grandparents set the bread to cook in a big heavy pan, covered with a lid, over a log fire. When it was baked they put it on a windowsill to cool.

Ingredients:

1 lb flour   **500 g**   4 cups
pinch of salt
½ teaspoon breadsoda
½ pint buttermilk or sour milk   **275 ml**   1¼ cups

Method:
1. Put the breadsoda into the palm of the hand and work with the back of a spoon to get rid of lumps. Add to the sieved flour and salt.
2. Make and bake as for speedy bread.

18

BROWN SODA BREAD

Ingredients:

10 oz plain flour	**275 g**	2½ cups
pinch of salt		
6 oz wholemeal flour	**175 g**	1 cup
½ teaspoon breadsoda		
½ pint buttermilk or sour milk	**275 ml**	1¼ cups

Method:

1. Sieve flour and salt into a bowl, add the wholemeal and baking soda.

2. Continue as for making and baking of speedy bread.

GRIDDLE BREAD

Griddle bread has been going strong in Ireland for centuries. A little effort produces a hot cake which makes splendid eating when spread thick with butter and smothered with honey or jam.

Ingredients:

8 oz flour	**225 g**	2 cups
pinch of salt		
1 teaspoon baking powder		
1 oz sugar	**25 g**	1½ tbsp.
1 oz melted butter	**25 g**	1½ tbsp.
¼ pint milk	**150 ml**	¾ cup
1 beaten egg		

Preparation time: 10 minutes   **Cooking time:** 15 minutes

Method:

1. Grease lightly a heavy iron pan.
2. Sieve the flour, salt and baking powder into a bowl; add in the sugar.
3. Add butter, milk and egg to the dry ingredients and mix well together.
4. Heat the greased pan and cook for 7 to 8 minutes, on each side over a moderate heat.
5. Divide into 4 to 8 triangular shapes and serve hot with with plenty of butter and jam or honey.

OATEN BREAD

Ingredients:

6 oz oatmeal	**175 g**	1 cup
½ pint buttermilk	**275 ml**	1¼ cups
10 oz plain flour	**275 g**	2½ cups
1 teaspoon salt		
1 level teaspoon breadsoda		

Preparation time: 10 minutes   **Cooking time:** 30–35 minutes

Oven position: top   **Oven temperature:** gas 6, 200°C, 400°F

Method:

1. Steep oatmeal in buttermilk for 5 minutes.
2. Sieve flour and salt into a bowl. Put baking soda into palm of hand and work with the back of spoon to get rid of lumps. Add to the sieved flour and salt.
3. Add in the soaked oatmeal. Mix well together.
4. Knead until smooth. Roll out, place on lightly floured baking sheet, and bake.
5. Cool on a wire tray.

YEAST BREAD

Ingredients:

½ oz fresh yeast (or 1 teaspoon dried yeast)	**15 g**	1 tbsp.
1 oz sugar	**25 g**	1½ tbsp.
2 tablespoons tepid water		
1 lb flour	**500 g**	4 cups
½ teaspoon salt		
1 oz butter or margarine	**25 g**	1½ tbsp.
½ pint milk	**275 ml**	1¼ cups

Preparation time: 15 minutes   **Cooking time:** 30–40 minutes
Proving time: 1 hour
Oven position: top   **Oven temperature:** gas 6, 200°C, 400°F

Method:

1. Put yeast, sugar and tepid water into a cup and stir to a cream, leave in a warm place for 10 minutes.
2. Have the mixing bowl warm. Sieve the flour and salt into it and keep in warm place.
3. Cut margarine or butter into small pieces, put with milk into a saucepan and heat over a gentle heat until the milk is tepid.
4. Pour yeast mixture into the flour. Add almost all the milk and mix thoroughly together until the dough is firm and elastic, adding more tepid milk if necessary.
5. Turn dough onto a floured board and knead for 5 to 10 minutes until smooth.
6. When the dough is smooth place in a floured bowl and cover with a damp cloth or tea towel. Leave for 25 minutes in a warm place.
7. When the dough has risen to double its size, knead again for five minutes. Put into a floured loaf tin, cover with a damp cloth and leave in a warm place for 30 to 35 minutes.
8. Brush top of loaf with a little milk mixture.

9. Place in oven. When baked set out on a wire rack to cool.

SODA APPLE CAKE

This is a very old recipe and for a cake that was typically made in the autumn—a way of using up the apples in the big country orchards. Surplus cooking apples were picked off the trees, each carefully wrapped in newspapers and stored away in a big box. Apples that had been very bitter in September would mature and become nice and sweet by Christmas.

Ingredients:

1 lb flour	**500 g**	4 cups
pinch of salt		
½ teaspoon breadsoda		
½ pint buttermilk	**275 ml**	1¼ cups
2-3 smallish apples peeled and sliced		
½ oz sugar	**15 g**	1 tbsp.

Preparation time: 15 minutes   **Cooking time:** 40–45 minutes
Oven position: top   **Oven temperature:** gas 6, 200°C, 400°F

Method:

1. Sieve flour, salt and baking soda into a bowl.
2. Make a well in the centre and add almost all the milk, mix to a loose dough, adding more liquid if necessary.
3. Turn on to a floured board and knead until smooth.
4. Cut mixture in half and roll each half out to fit round 9-inch tin.
5. Flour the tin lightly. Place one circle of dough in the tin, arrange apples on dough, sprinkle with sugar, cover with remaining dough. Put tin in the oven.
6. When baked, turn cake on to a wire rack to cool.

To vary:

Add some mixed spice or cinnamon; dried fruit, like raisins or currants, may also be sprinkled on top of the apples.

BREAKFAST SCONES

The Irish seem to have decided long ago that, since nature had given them rich butter, honey and jam, they would have to provide a properly royal platter for these good things. This handy platter is the scone: a wholemeal confection unsurpassed in thick wholesomeness, giving healthy bulk to the first meal of the day.

Ingredients:

6 oz flour	**175 g**	1½ cups

pinch of salt

2 oz wholemeal flour	**50 g**	1/3 cup
1 oz butter or margarine	**25 g**	1 1/2 tbsp.
1 teaspoon baking powder		
2 tablespoons golden syrup		
1/4 pint milk	**150 ml**	5/8 cup
3 oz bran (optional)	**75 g**	3/4 cup

Preparation time: 10 minutes   **Cooking time:** 20–25 minutes
Oven position: top   **Oven temperature:** gas 6, 200°C, 400°F

Method:

1. Sieve flour and salt into a bowl, add wholemeal and bran if used.
2. Put in the margarine or butter, add the baking powder, mix ingredients well together.
3. Add the syrup and enough milk to mix to a loose dough. Add extra milk if bran is used.
4. Turn onto a floured board and knead until smooth. Roll out, cut the dough in half, then into quarters and then into eighths.
5. Place on a lightly floured baking sheet and place in the oven.
6. When baked, set out on a wire rack to cool.

HONEY SCONES

Make as for breakfast scones but substitute 2 tablespoons of honey in place of syrup.

FRUIT SCONES

Ingredients:

8 oz flour	**225 g**	2 cups
pinch of salt		
1 oz butter or margarine	**25 g**	1 1/2 tbsp.
1 oz sugar	**25 g**	1 1/2 tbsp.
1 teaspoon baking powder		
2 oz raisins	**50 g**	2/3 cup
2 oz chopped dates	**50 g**	2/3 cup
1/4 pint sweet milk approximately	**150 ml**	5/8 cup

Preparation time: 15 minutes   **Cooking time:** 25 minutes
Oven position: top   **Oven temperature:** gas 6, 200°C, 400°F

Method:

1. Sieve flour and salt into a bowl, rub in the fat, add the sugar, baking powder and fruit and mix well together.
2. Add liquid and continue as for breakfast scones.

22

To vary:

Take an orange, grate it and squeeze the juice. Add the rind and a little juice to the dry ingredients. Less milk will be required.

OAT CAKES

Oatmeal has long been a staple food of the Irish. These rich and tasty cakes were usually cooked on a big, heavy, flat well-greased sheet over a peat or log fire. Today they are normally baked in the oven.

Ingredients:

8 oz Oatmeal	**225 g**	1⅓ cups
4 oz plain flour	**100 g**	1 cup
pinch of salt		
pinch of breadsoda		
2 oz margarine	**50 g**	3 tbsp.
hot water		

Preparation time: 15 minutes   **Cooking time:** 20 minutes
Oven position: top   **Oven temperature:** gas 6, 200°C, 400°F

Method:

1. Put oatmeal into a bowl.
2. Sieve flour, salt and breadsoda into the same bowl.
3. Melt the margarine and add to the dry ingredients.
4. Add enough hot water to make a firm dough.
5. Sprinkle a worktop with oatmeal and roll out dough.
6. Cut into rounds, using a tea cup, arrange on a greased baking sheet and bake for 20 minutes.
7. Cool on a wire tray.
8. When cooled, serve.

IRISH BUTTER

"Butter is the cream," according to an advertisement on Irish television. And it is—18 pints of milk are needed to get a pound of butter.

The dairy at home was a little building attached to the main house; it had its own outside entrance. Not only butter but milk, skim milk, cream, buttermilk and eggs were prepared and stored here.

When the cows were milked, their milk was brought to the dairy, where it was separated. The cream passed through a funnel on one side of the separator; skimmed, creamless milk passed through a funnel on the other side.

At home we generally drank whole milk at breakfast, tea and supper and skim milk with our midday meal. The rest of the skim milk was given to the calves, pigs and hens.

Appetizers

COUNTRY PÂTÉ

Pâtés originally were invented, it seems, to use up leftover and cheaper cuts of meat. Eventually they became a culinary art form in themselves.

Many a good French restaurant has built a substantial reputation owing to a good start with an original pâté or terrine. The Irish, whose pâtés used to be imported, have now taken up the challenge, and a number of Irish chefs have invented splendid native variants. Here is my own humbler contribution.

Ingredients:

6 streaky rashers		
1 lb chicken livers	**500 g**	2 cups
2 tablespoons oil		
1 large onion (finely chopped)		
2 cloves crushed garlic		
8 oz sausage meat	**225 g**	1 cup
1 small red and 1 small green pepper		
seeded and finely chopped		
1 tablespoon finely chopped fresh		
mint		
2 tablespoons brandy		
seasoning		
watercress		

Preparation time: 20 minutes
Oven position: centre

Cooking time: 1 hour
Oven temperature:
gas 6, 200°C, 400°F

Method:

1. Rinse chicken livers under cold water, then steep in salted tepid water for 15 minutes. Rinse in cold water.
2. Line a loaf tin with streaky rashers.
3. Heat the oil and fry the chicken livers for 5 minutes.
4. Add onions, garlic, sausage meat, peppers and mint and continue cooking for a further 5 minutes.
5. Allow to cool, liquidize (using blender if available) and put mixture through a sieve.
6. Add brandy (if used) and season to taste.
7. Put into rasher-lined loaf tin.
8. Stand the loaf tin in a deep tin half filled with boiling water. Cover tin with tinfoil. Set in oven and bake.
9. When baked turn onto serving plate; garnish with watercress.

MACKEREL TERRINE

Ingredients:

Serves: 4

8 oz cooked mackerel	225 g	1 cup	
¼ pint milk	150 ml	½ cup	
1 oz butter or margarine	25 g	1½ tbsp.	
1 oz flour	25 g	¼ cup	
2 eggs			
finely chopped parsley			
lemon wedges			

Preparation time: 15 minutes   **Cooking time:** 20 minutes

1. Hard boil the eggs.
2. Remove skin and bones from the mackerel.
3. Put mackerel into a saucepan with milk and nutmeg. Bring to the boil and simmer until tender (15 to 20 minutes).
4. Remove the fish and retain the flavoured milk.
5. Melt the butter or margarine for a minute, add the flour and beat with a wooden spoon over a gentle heat. Gradually add the flavoured milk. Bring to the boil.
6. Remove shells from the hard-boiled eggs and sieve.
7. Combine all ingredients and beat well.
8. Pile into serving dish; garnish with parsley and lemon wedges.

To vary:

Take the rind and juice of an orange. Combine orange juice and enough milk to make up half cup of liquid specified in recipe. Add the orange rind to the sauce along with remaining ingredients.

Note: Tinned mackerel may be used.

PRAWN COCKTAIL

Prawns have been a very popular starter over the years, and are particularly good when jumbo prawns are available. Mixed with a nice homemade mayonnaise and a little cream, they make a delightful overture to any dinner party.

Ingredients:

Serves: 4

8 lettuce leaves		
1 lb shelled cooked prawn meat	500 g	2 cups
1 lb cooked shrimp meat	500 g	2 cups
½ pint mayonnaise	275 ml	1¼ cups
1–2 tablespoons cream		
1–2 tablespoons tomato purée		
seasoning		
lemon wedges		

paprika

Preparation time: 20–25 minutes

Method:

1. Wash and shred lettuce leaves and arrange half of them in the bottom of 4 cocktail glasses.
2. Arrange half the fish on top of lettuce.
3. Mix mayonnaise, cream, tomato purée together, and season to taste.
4. Pour half the mayonnaise over the fish.
5. Continue with a second and, if desired, a third layer of lettuce, shrimp and mayonnaise.
6. Garnish with lemon wedges. Sprinkle with a little paprika.

To vary:

Take a grapefruit, cut it in half, scoop out the flesh and chop. Only half the number of shrimp will be needed. Mix all the ingredients together and pile back into the half shell of grapefruit.

Watchpoint:

Shrimp should always be cooked when very fresh.

BUTTERED COCKLES

There are cockle beaches all round the coast of Ireland. People living nearby will collect bucketfuls of cockles, return home and wash them several times to remove the sand. Then they put them into a saucepan without any other liquid other than that from the shells. They cook them for five minutes or so, then strain away the liquid and eat them on their own without any bread or salad.

Ingredients: Serves: 3–4

2 dozen cockles
2 oz butter   **50 g**   3 tbsp.
finely chopped parsley
seasoning
buttered brown scones (to serve)

Preparation time: 10 minutes   Cooking time: 4–5 minutes

Method:

1. Wash and scrub cockle shells well in cold water, put into saucepan and cook for 4 to 5 minutes over a gentle heat.
2. Strain off liquid and remove shells.
3. Heat the butter in a saucepan, add fish and parsley and heat through for a minute. Turn onto serving dish.
4. Serve piping hot with buttered brown scones.

26

SALMON FINGERS

Salmon was a luxury in our house. We'd have it three or four times during the summer. Mother would poach the salmon and serve it with brown soda bread.

Salmon fingers make good appetizers, and are ideal for buffet parties because they can be made and filled in advance.

Ingredients: Serves: 10

filling:

¼ pint choux pastry	**150 ml**	⅝ cup
4 oz salmon	**100 g**	½ cup

6 leaves lettuce (washed and
   shredded)
1 finely sliced tomato
1 hard-boiled chopped egg
8 slices chopped cucumber
2–3 scallions (washed and chopped)
1 mashed hard-boiled egg
seasoning
2–3 tablespoons mayonnaise

to coat:

¼ pint mayonnaise	**150 ml**	⅝ cup

cayenne pepper
slices of tomato and cucumber

Preparation time: 20 minutes   **Cooking time:** 25 minutes
Oven position: top   **Oven temperature:** gas 6, 200°C, 400°F

Method:

1. Make choux pastry (see page 133). Pipe 10 to 12 eclairs onto a greased baking sheet.
2. Prepare all filling ingredients. Mix well together, season to taste and mix with mayonnaise.
3. Divide the filling evenly among eclairs and stuff each eclair shell with filling.
4. Arrange filled eclair on serving plate.
5. Coat each eclair with mayonnaise, sprinkle a little cayenne pepper on top.
6. Garnish with slices of tomato and cucumber.

To vary:

Make filling with a white panard sauce, and add any cooked meat, fish or vegetables desired.

SALMON QUICHE

Salmon quiche is a very rich dish which can be used as an appetizer or served as an entrée at lunch with plenty of fresh vegetables. Because it is so filling, it is

27

best served in small pieces.

Ingredients: **Serves: 6**

pastry:

6 oz flour	**175 g**	$\frac{5}{8}$ cup
pinch of salt		
3 oz margarine	**75 g**	$\frac{3}{8}$ cup
cold water		

filling:

$\frac{1}{2}$ oz margarine	**15 g**	1 tbsp.
$\frac{1}{2}$ medium-sized onion (finely chopped)		
$3\frac{1}{2}$ oz tin salmon or fresh salmon	**100 g**	$\frac{1}{2}$ cup
2 tomatoes		
2 eggs and 1 egg yolk		
2 oz grated cheddar cheese	**50 g**	$\frac{1}{2}$ cup
salt and pepper		
$\frac{1}{2}$ pint cream or milk	**275 ml**	$1\frac{1}{4}$ cups

Preparation time: 20 minutes   **Cooking time:** 25–30 minutes
Oven position: centre   **Oven temperature:**
gas 6, 200°C, 400°F

Method for preparing:

1. Sieve flour and salt into a bowl.
2. Add margarine, cutting it into small pieces, then rubbing it into flour with tips of fingers until mixture resembles fine breadcrumbs.
3. Add enough cold water (approximately 3 tablespoons) to bind, and mix to a fairly stiff dough.
4. Turn out onto a floured board and knead lightly.
5. Roll out and line 9-inch flan ring (set on a baking sheet).
6. Bake pastry shell unfilled (but cover pastry with sheet of brown or greaseproof paper and cover that with uncooked rice or macaroni). Bake in the oven for 10 minutes.
7. Remove rice or macaroni and paper, and fill with savoury filling.

Method for preparing filling:

1. In the meantime, melt margarine and gently fry onion for 1 to 2 minutes.
2. Drain tin of salmon, discard bone and flake fish with fork.
3. Put tomatoes into a bowl, pour boiling water over them, leave one minute and remove skins, slice and remove seeds.
4. Arrange onion, tomato and salmon in flan case.
5. Beat eggs and egg yolk, add cheese and cream then season to taste.
6. Place egg mixture over salmon mixture in pastry shell.
7. Place in the oven and bake for 25 minutes.

to prevent sauce from becoming bitter.

CRAB PUFFS

Ingredients: Serves: 10

¼ pint choux pastry	**150 ml**	⅝ cup	
filling:			
1 lb cooked crab meat	**500 g**	2 cups	
2–3 tablespoons cream			
¼ pint mayonnaise	**150 ml**	⅝ cup	
4 oz washed and seeded			
green grapes	**100 g**	1⅓ cups	
seasoning			

Preparation time: 20 minutes   **Cooking time:** 25 minutes
Oven position: top   **Oven temperature:** gas 6, 200°C, 400°F

Method for preparing puffs:

1. Make choux pastry.
2. Pipe or spoon choux buns (roughly two inches in diameter) onto a greased baking sheet.
3. Put into the oven and bake for 25 minutes.

Method of preparing filling:

1. Chop crabmeat.
2. Mix the cream, mayonnaise, crab and half the grapes together, add seasoning to taste.
3. Pile this mixture into the choux buns.
4. Arrange on serving dish and decorate with remaining grapes.

Watchpoint:

With crab it is best to blend white and brown meat. Use one part white meat to half part brown meat. Buy crabs that are heavy in proportion to size as they contain more meat. Medium to large-sized crabs are best.

BATTER AND PANCAKES

Most Irish country people associate batter and pancakes with Shrove Tuesday, which we called Pancake Tuesday because it was a day we spent a lot of time making batters and pancakes. We used to sprinkle the pancakes with sugar and serve them hot with a lemon sauce. Today we serve them with all kinds of sweet or savoury fillings or sauces.

Ingredients: Serves: 4–6

4 oz flour	**100 g**	1 cup
pinch of salt		
1 egg		
1 oz melted butter	**25 g**	1½ tbsp.
½ pint milk	**275 ml**	1¼ cups
1 oz margarine	**25 g**	1½ tbsp.

lemon wedges
a little castor sugar

Preparation time: 10 minutes (rest time for batter: 2 hours)
Cooking time: 10 minutes

Method for making batter:

1. Sieve flour and salt into a bowl.
2. Make a well in the centre and drop in egg, melted margarine and half the milk.
3. Beat with a wooden spoon, gradually drawing in the flour from the sides of the bowl; beat well to form a smooth batter.
4. Beat in the remaining milk, cover and let stand for 2 hours.

Method for making pancakes:

1. Melt margarine in a medium size frying pan. Pour off excess margarine and just leave it lightly greased.
2. Pour in enough batter to make a very thin coating in the pan, and cook until underside is golden brown.
3. Toss or turn the pancake and cook until the other side is golden brown.
4. Sprinkle with sugar, loosely roll up.
5. Keep warm until ready to serve. Garnish with lemon wedges.

CRAWFISH PANCAKES

The crawfish, called crayfish in many parts of America, is not unlike the lobster. Though much bigger, it has no large front claw. In Ireland crawfish are in season all year round but are most plentiful during the summer months.

Ingredients: Serves: 4–6

1 lb crawfish meat	**500 g**	2 cups
½ pint white wine	**275 ml**	1¼ cups
1 oz butter	**25 g**	1½ tbsp.
a few peppercorns		
1 finely chopped onion		
1 oz flour	**25 g**	¼ cup
finely chopped parsley		
2 oz grated cheese	**50 g**	½ cup
2–3 tablespoons cream		

Preparation time: 20 minutes   **Cooking time:** 30–40 minutes

Method:

1. Make pancakes and keep hot. Layer pancakes and place a sheet of greaseproof paper between each one. Cover over completely with greaseproof paper and place in a warm oven.
2. Cook the crawfish in boiling salted water for 30 to 40 minutes. Remove flesh from shell after cooking.
3. Put wine and peppercorns into a saucepan and reduce by

half—i.e., boil over a fast heat until half the wine has evaporated. Strain and reserve remaining wine.

4. Melt butter and fry onions over a gentle heat for 2 minutes or so until transparent. Add the flour and cook for a further minute.
5. Gradually add the wine, chopped parsley and fish, bring to the boil, then remove from heat.
6. Add cheese and cream.

7. Divide the filling evenly between the pancakes and roll them up.
8. Serve hot, garnished with finely chopped parsley.

To vary:
Garnish using fresh seasonal vegetables.

To economize:
Use fish stock or milk instead of wine.

POTTED HERRINGS

Herring is a very popular fish here in Ireland. Fifteen to twenty years ago it was possible to buy a dozen herrings fresh from the sea for only two shillings.

Ingredients: Serves: 6

6 freshly filleted herrings		
½ pint white wine vinegar	**275 ml**	1¼ cups
½ pint water	**275 ml**	1¼ cups
2 bay leaves		
1 finely chopped onion		
5 or 6 peppercorns		
½ teaspoon mustard seeds		
buttered slices of brown bread (to serve)		

Preparation time: 10 minutes   **Resting time:** 2–3 days

Method:
1. Sprinkle fillets with salt and leave to drain for 3 hours.
2. Roll up each fillet from head to tail and secure with a skewer or cocktail stick.
3. Pack them into an oval-shaped casserole.
4. Put remaining ingredients into a saucepan and bring to the boil

and simmer for 5 minutes. Allow to cool.
5. Strain and pour liquid over fillets of herring.
6. Cover and place in the bottom of refrigerator for at least 2 days.
7. Serve with buttered slices of brown soda bread.

DRESSED EEL

Ingredients: Serves: 6

1 lb eel	**500 g**	2 cups
½ pint white wine	**275 ml**	1¼ cups
1 finely chopped onion		

31

bay leaf
a few peppercorns
egg and fine breadcrumbs
fat for deep frying
finely chopped parsley
lemon wedges

Preparation time: 10 minutes   **Cooking time:** 5 minutes
Resting time: 2–3 hours

Method:

1. Cut the prepared eel into pieces about 2 inches long.
2. Put into a bowl and pour wine over, add onion, bay leaf and peppercorns, cover and leave for 2–3 hours.
3. Put into a saucepan and cook over a gentle heat for 5 minutes.
4. Drain fish, reserving flavoured wine. Allow time to cool.

over a gentle heat for 5
5. Coat fish with egg and breadcrumbs and fry in hot fat.
6. Drain well on kitchen paper.
7. Make coating sauce, substituting flavoured wine in place of milk.
8. Serve with garnish of parsley and lemon wedges.

SWEETBREAD RINGS

In days gone by sweetbreads were a favourite with the Irish poor because they were inexpensive and made a very appetizing dish.

A whole sweetbread—the thymus gland of a calf—weighs, conveniently, about a pound. There are two lobes, one of them smooth, round and solid; this is the choicest piece. The other, called the throat sweetbread, has an uneven shape; it is broken by viens and often slit.

Ingredients: Serves: 6–8

¼ pint choux pastry	**150 ml**	1¼ cups
filling:		
½ lb lamb sweetbreads	**225 g**	1 cup
2–3 slices of lemon or a few drops of vinegar		
4 oz sliced mushrooms	**100 g**	¾ cup
1 tablespoon butter or margarine		
4 oz cooked ham	**100 g**	⅔ cup
sauce: 1 oz butter or margarine	**25 g**	1½ tbsp.
1½ oz flour	**40 g**	⅓ cup
½ pint stock from sweetbreads	**275 ml**	1¼ cups
chopped parsley		

Preparation time: 30 minutes   **Cooking time:** 25 minutes
Oven position: top   **Oven temperature:** gas 6, 200°C, 400°F

Method for choux rings:
1. Make choux pastry.
2. Pipe rings of 2 inches in diameter at base onto a greased baking sheet.
3. Bake for 25 minutes.

Method for preparing sweetbreads:
1. Soak the sweetbreads for twenty minutes in salted tepid water, then rinse them under the cold tap. Put them into a pan of cold water with a pinch of salt, a slice of lemon or a few drops of vinegar, and bring them slowly to the boil. Remove any scum, as it raises to the surface. Simmer for 25 minutes.
2. Strain sweetbreads, reserving the liquid for the sauce. Rinse them quickly, remove any skin, and press them between two plates. Put a weight on top to remove any excess liquid, leave until cold; strain and cut into small pieces.

Method for preparing filling with sauce:
1. Fry mushrooms gently in 1 tablespoon butter or margarine for 3 or 4 minutes.
2. Make the sauce, melt butter or margarine. Remove from the heat, add the flour and mix well together. Add the liquid gradually, stirring all the time.
3. Add the sweetbreads, mushrooms, ham and season to taste, bring just to boiling point. Allow to cool.
4. Split the rings horizontally and put a good spoonful of filling inside. Cover and put remaining filling into centre of ring.
5. Sprinkle with parsley and serve hot.

POACHED EGG MAYONNAISE
Ingredients: Serves: 4

4 eggs
5–6 leaves of lettuce
$\frac{1}{2}$ cup mayonnaise
cayenne pepper
parsley sprigs

Preparation time: 20 minutes   **Cooking time:** 3 minutes

Method:
1. Poach eggs carefully for 3 minutes. Remove and put in a bowl of cold water.
2. Arrange lettuce on a serving dish.
3. Drain and dry eggs and set on bed of lettuce.
4. Spoon mayonnaise over eggs and sprinkle with cayenne pepper.
5. Decorate with sprigs of parsley.

AIRY MUSHROOMS
As children we loved going to the fields to pick wild mushrooms. We were taught to check the colour underneath the cap; if they were black we had to

33

discard them.

The black ones were supposed to be fairies in disguise. What they were in fact were mushrooms too old to eat.

When we got home we would put the fresh mushrooms in a big dish. When mother was out of the kitchen we'd usually manage to sneak two or three, skin them, season them, and put them on the oven floor for a minute with a lump of butter on each. Then we'd nip off to a corner of the front garden to eat them.

This recipe is for a mushroom soufflé.

Ingredients: Serves: 4

1 oz melted margarine	**25 g**	1½ tbsp.
2 oz fine brown breadcrumbs	**50 g**	1 cup
1 oz margarine	**25 g**	1½ tbsp.
1 oz flour	**25 g**	¼ cup
¼ pint milk	**150 ml**	⅝ cup
4 egg yolks		
5 oz chopped mushrooms	**150 g**	1 cup
seasoning		
5 egg whites		

Preparation time: 20 minutes **Cooking time:** 35–45 minutes
Oven position: centre   **Oven temperature:**
gas 5, 190°C, 375°F

Method:

1. Prepare a 1½ pint (3 cup) soufflé case by greasing with melted margarine, then dust with breadcrumbs.
2. Cut out a double sheet of brown or greaseproof paper, 1½ times the depth of soufflé case allowing an inch on the width to overlap.
3. Tie this strip around the outer edge of soufflé dish and grease the paper well.
4. Melt the margarine, add flour and stir well; gradually add the milk and stir continuously until it reaches boiling point.
5. Add the yolks, one at a time; add mushrooms and season to taste. Allow to cool.
6. Beat the egg whites until firm. Add a tablespoonful to the sauce, then quickly fold in the remainder. Turn mixture into prepared case. Set into the oven and cook for 35 to 45 minutes.
7. When cooking is done, remove paper from outside the case. Serve immediately.

STUFFED TOMATO WHEEL

It would be hard to improve on the flavour of fresh Irish tomatoes. July and August are the best months for them. The quality of our best greenhouse tomatoes is far superior in flavour and texture to any of the imported varieties.

Irish tomatoes are very firm and so are ideal for stuffing. And stuffed tomatoes provide an ideal way of using up leftover meat, fish or vegetables.

Ingredients: Serves: 4

4 large tomatoes
2 medium-sized cooked potatoes
1 tablespoon cooked peas
1 teaspoon chopped herbs
seasoning
mayonnaise
4 pineapple rings
finely chopped herbs

Preparation time: 15 minutes

Method:
1. Cut tops from rounded ends of tomatoes. Scoop out the flesh and put through a sieve.
2. Cut the potatoes into cubes, add sieved flesh, peas, herbs, seasoning and mayonnaise to taste. Spoon this filling into the tomatoes.
3. Place pineapple rings on individual serving plates, arrange the tomatoes on top and sprinkle with herbs.

To vary:
Serve hot, omitting pineapple rings, perhaps grating some cheese over the top of tomato. Bake in moderate oven for 10 to 15 minutes.

WEIGHTS AND MEASURES

An important point to remember with regard to solid measures. Irish cooks are generous with their teaspoon and tablespoon measures: these are usually heaped, while the American cook levels off the quantity on the spoon with a knife. So it is important to note that where a recipe specifies a teaspoon of sugar, for example, you should use a rounded teaspoonful, i.e. as much above the spoon as in it, or **two** level teaspoonfuls.

Stocks

A good foundation is needed to build a good soup or sauce. That's what a good stock is for. Stocks can be made in large quantities and stored for four or five days in a refrigerator or for a few months in a freezer.

When making stock, it is important to extract all the flavoursome juices. This is done by prolonged slow cooking over a gentle heat. Stock made from aged animal meat and mature vegetables will have more flavour than stock made from young and tender meat and vegetables.

HINTS ON STOCKMAKING

1. Put all the ingredients in a saucepan and cover with cold water, bring gently to the boil. Simmer for at least 3 or 4 hours.
2. As the stock heats, heavy scum rises to the surface. Remove this scum to obtain a clear stock.
3. When stock is cooked, let it cool, then cover it tightly and refrigerate or freeze it.

As it cools, the grease will form a solid mass of fat on top. This serves to protect it. So don't remove this layer of fat until you are ready to reheat the stock for use.

Watchpoints:

Raw and cooked bones should not be mixed. Don't use gravy in any stock. Starchy foods tend to make the stock spoil rapidly.

STOCKPOT

A special pot should be kept for stockmaking—ideally a pot with a tap, so that the liquid can be drawn off and the vegetables and bones held back.

The bones:

These should be broken up into small pieces and browned in the oven without fat before being put into the stockpot. The procedure will improve the colour of the stock.

The vegetables:

To improve flavour and colour, brown vegetables in a little fat before adding to the stockpot.

The seasoning:

Use salt sparingly; too much can ruin a good stock. If stock is to be stored for some time the salt taste is likely to intensify. Use herbs sparingly, too.

BONE STOCK
Ingredients:

6½ lbs marrow bones	**3 kg**	
4 quarts cold water	**5 litres**	
6 cloves		
1 chopped onion		
2 diced stalks celery		
2 chopped carrots		
3 sprigs parsley		
1 bay leaf		
1 teaspoon thyme		

Preparation time: 15 minutes   **Cooking time:** 3 hours

Method:

1. Break bones into small pieces and brown in the oven.
2. Put into stockpot and cover with cold water.
3. Stick the cloves into onion and add, with remaining ingredients to stock pot.
4. Bring to the boil over gentle heat.
5. Simmer for 2½ to 3 hours uncovered.
6. Strain stock and cool uncovered, then cover and refrigerate or freeze.

LIGHT STOCK
Ingredients:

3½ lb veal bones	**1.5 kg**	
2 quarts cold water	**2.5 litres**	
1 chopped onion		
3 chopped sticks celery		
2 chopped carrots		
6 white peppercorns		
1 bay leaf		

Preparation time: 15 minutes   **Cooking time:** 3 hours

Method:

1. Put all ingredients into the stockpot.
2. Bring to the boil and simmer gently for 2½ to 3 hours.
3. Strain stock, cool, cover and refrigerate or freeze.

Note:

Used for soups and sauces.

FISH STOCK
Ingredients:

2 oz margarine	**50 g**		¼ cup

2 chopped onions	
2 chopped carrots	
2 chopped sticks celery	
6 white peppercorns	
2 tablespoons vinegar	
2 quarts water	**2.5 litres**
1 tablespoon lemon juice	
2 lbs fish bones	**1 kg**

Preparation time: 15 minutes   Cooking time: 20–25 minutes

Method:

1. Heat the fat, add diced vegetables and cook for a few minutes.
2. Add remaining ingredients.
3. Bring gently to the boil; continue cooking uncovered over a brisk heat for 20–25 minutes only; it will become bitter if left any longer.
4. Strain and cool; cover and refrigerate or freeze.

BEEF STOCK

Ingredients:

2 lbs neck of beef bones	**1 kg**
4 quarts water	**5 litres**
2 chopped carrots	
2 chopped leeks	
3 chopped sticks celery	
3 chopped onions	
bouquet garni	

Preparation time: 15 minutes   Cooking time: 2½ hours

Method:

1. Put meat and bones into the stock pot; cover with cold water and bring gently to the boil over a low heat.
2. Add vegetables; cover partially and continue cooking over a gentle heat for 2 hours.
3. Strain and cool; cover and refrigerate or freeze.

CHICKEN STOCK 1

Ingredients:

4 lbs chicken necks, wings, fat	**2 kg**
4 quarts cold water	**5 litres**
1 chopped onion	
3 chopped sticks celery	

2 chopped carrots
6 white peppercorns
1 bay leaf
1 teaspoon fresh thyme

Preparation time: 15 minutes   **Cooking time:** 3 hours

Method:
Prepare and store as for light
stock.

CHICKEN STOCK 2

Ingredients:

chicken bones
giblets from chicken (omitting liver)
3 chopped carrots
3 chopped onions
3 chopped sticks celery
3 pints water   **1.5 litres**
parsley stalks
bay leaf
a few peppercorns
tomato and mushroom skins

Preparation time: 15 minutes   **Cooking time:** 3 hours

Method:
1. Put bones, giblets, vegetables, water and seasonings into a saucepan.
2. Bring to the boil over a gentle heat.
3. Simmer for at least 2 to 3 hours.
4. Strain and cool; cover and refrigerate or freeze.

GAME STOCK

Ingredients:

4 lbs fowl or rabbit bones   **2 kg**
4 quarts cold water   **5 litres**
1 chopped onion
3 chopped celery sticks
2 chopped carrots
4–5 sprigs parsley
bay leaf

Preparation time: 15 minutes   **Cooking time:** 3 hours

Method:

Prepare and store as for light stock, using the above ingredients.

VEGETABLE STOCK

Ingredients:

2 oz margarine	**50 g**	¼ cup
3 oz chopped onion	**75 g**	¾ cup
1 teaspoon sugar		
1 teaspoon fresh thyme		
6 black peppercorns		
3 oz chopped parsnip	**75 g**	¾ cup
3 oz white turnip	**75 g**	¾ cup
6 oz chopped carrot	**175 g**	1½ cups
6 oz chopped celery	**175 g**	1½ cups
2 quarts water	**2.5 litres**	

Preparation time: 15 minutes   **Cooking time:** 2 hours

Method:

1. Heat margarine; fry the onion in it gently until it turns a rich brown colour.
2. Add sugar and vegetables; cook for 3–4 minutes.
3. Cover with cold water, bring to boil over a gentle heat.
4. Cover partially and simmer for 1½ hours.
5. Strain and cool; cover and refrigerate or freeze.

WEIGHTS AND MEASURES

An important point to remember with regard to solid measures. Irish cooks are generous with their teaspoon and tablespoon measures: these are usually heaped, while the American cook levels off the quantity on the spoon with a knife. So it is important to note that where a recipe specifies a teaspoon of sugar, for example, you should use a rounded teaspoonful, i.e. as much above the spoon as in it, or **two** level teaspoonfuls.

Soups

COCKLE SOUP

In the late nineteenth century, shellfish was a staple in the diet of poor people living around the coast. Today shellfish is considered a luxury for the rich—high quality food fresh from the sea. Yet even the poorer Irish, if they live near the coast, still take the availability of shellfish for granted.

Ingredients: Serves: 4–6

2 dozen cockles		
1 oz butter	**25 g**	1½ tbsp.
2 peeled and diced potatoes		
2 finely chopped onions		
2 finely chopped sticks celery		
1 pint fish stock or water	**575 ml**	2½ cups
1 pint milk	**575 ml**	2½ cups
salt and pepper		
2–3 tablespoons lightly whipped cream		

Preparation time: 30 minutes   **Cooking time:** 25 minutes

Method:

1. Wash and scrub the cockles well and put into basin of cold water and leave for 20 minutes.
2. Heat the butter in a saucepan, add the vegetables and cook for a minute.
3. Add the milk and stock or water and bring to the boil. Then simmer for 20 minutes.
4. Add the cockles; shortly afterwards they will open.
5. Remove shells.
6. Season to taste.
7. Serve hot topped with cream.

MUSSEL CHOWDER

In Ireland mussels are gathered at low tide, by hand, or using rakes or dredges. Mussels, are found all year round. Sea farming or aquaculture today concentrates mainly on harvesting salmon, trout, mussels and oysters. Of these mussels are easiest to cultivate: seeding can be done at little or no cost; the growing period is short; harvesting requires only simple and inexpensive equipment.

Ingredients: Serves: 4–6

2 dozen mussels		
1 oz butter or margarine	**25 g**	1½ tbsp.

2 finely chopped onions		
3 chopped tomatoes (with skins and seeds removed)		
3 diced potatoes		
1 apple (peeled, cored and chopped)		
1 pint fish stock	**575 ml**	2½ cups
1 oz cornflour blended with a little milk	**25 g**	2 tbsp.
½ pint milk	**275 ml**	1¼ cups
½ pint Guinness	**275 ml**	1¼ cups
tomato slices		

Preparation time: 15 minutes   **Cooking time:** 25 minutes

Method:

1. Wash mussels and let sit in fresh cold water.
2. Melt margarine or butter, add vegetables and cook for a minute. Add stock and milk.
3. Bring to the boil and simmer for 20 minutes.
4. Add mussels, blend cornstarch and Guinness. Cook for 5 minutes.
5. Remove mussel shells.
6. Serve garnished with tomato slices.

SCALLOP SOUP

Ingredients: Serves: 4

6 scallops		
1 oz butter or margarine	**25 g**	1½ tbsp.
2 oz lean diced bacon	**50 g**	⅓ cup
8 oz diced potatoes	**225 g**	2 cups
1 pint milk	**575 ml**	2½ cups
½ pint fish stock	**275 ml**	1¼ cups
4 oz seeded and sliced tomatoes	**100 g**	⅔ cup
a little mace		
salt and pepper		
a little cream		
finely chopped parsley		

Preparation time: 15 minutes   **Cooking time:** 30 minutes

Method:

1. Wash scallops in fresh cold water.
2. Melt fat in a large saucepan;
add bacon and potatoes and fry for a minute.
3. Add the milk and fish stock,

bring to the boil. Cover and simmer for 25 minutes.
4. Put the scallops into a saucepan and just cover with cold water, bring to the boil.
5. Strain reserve juice and remove shells. Chop the flesh.

6. Add scallop meat, juice, tomatoes and mace to milk and potatoes and season to taste.
7. Bring back to the boil and simmer for 3–5 minutes.
8. Serve hot, garnish with cream and chopped parsley.

WHITEFISH SOUP

Whitefish (whiting) live, like cod and haddock, near the bottom of the sea. Irish fishermen usually trawl for them, dragging a conical net bag along the seabed. The largest quantities are fished off the east and north-west coasts.

Until recently Catholics were obliged to abstain from meat on Fridays; whitefish soup was often a staple of the Friday diet.

Ingredients: Serves: 4–6

8 oz whiting, cod or haddock	**225 g**	1 cup
1 finely chopped large onion		
2 finely chopped parsnips		
1 pint fish stock or water	**575 ml**	2½ cups
1 pint milk	**575 ml**	2½ cups
seasoning		
lemon wedges		

Preparation time: 15 minutes   **Cooking time:** 20 minutes

Method:
1. Remove bones and skin from fish and cut up. The bones and skin can be used in making stock.
2. Put all ingredients into a sauce-

pan, bring to the boil, season to taste, and simmer for 20 minutes.
3. Serve hot, garnished with lemon wedges.

FISH CHOWDER

Some people like to say of a pint of Guinness that there's eating and drinking in it, but the saying really seems to have arisen in a halting and stumbling effort to describe the ineffable satisfactions of good chowder. Even when we were children we knew this was more than merely a soup; rightly made it could be a delicious main course dish.

For fish chowder almost any fish will do. Two Irish favourites are cod and haddock. Haddock is called St Peter's thumb because of the indentation the old fisherman is supposed to have made in its side.

Ingredients: Serves: 4

12 oz haddock or cod	**325 g**	1½ cups

2 oz butter or margarine	**50 g**	$\frac{1}{4}$ cup
2 diced onions		
1 lb peeled and diced potatoes	**500 g**	4 cups
3 chopped sticks celery		
1¾ pints stock	**1 litre**	4½ cups
bouquet garni		
salt and pepper		

Preparation time: 15 minutes   **Cooking time:** 30 minutes

Method:

1. Remove skin and bones from fish (these can be used in the making of fish stock).
2. Heat butter or margarine, add fish and vegetables and fry for a minute.
3. Add stock, bring to the boil; add bouquet garni and season to taste.
4. Cover and simmer for 25 to 30 minutes.
5. Serve piping hot.

BRACHAN CAOIREOLA

Pronounced, roughly, brawk-on care-rolla; this is mutton broth—one of the most traditional of Irish soups. Oatmeal was commonly used by the Irish to thicken soups already rich in flavour from meat bones: the older the bones the richer the flavour.

Ingredients: Serves: 4

½ lb neck of mutton	**225 g**	
1¾ pints water	**1 litre**	4½ cups
1 oz barley	**25 g**	$\frac{1}{4}$ cup
12 oz diced vegetables		
(carrots, onions, leeks, potatoes)	**325 g**	3 cups
bouquet garni		
seasoning		
finely chopped parsley		

Preparation time: 20 minutes   **Cooking time:** 2 hours

Method:

1. Wipe meat off with a damp cloth, remove spinal cord and put in a saucepan with water and barley. Bring to the boil and skim.
2. Add vegetables, bouquet garni, and season to taste.
3. Bring back to the boil, cover and simmer for 1½ to 2 hours.
4. Remove meat, check seasoning.
5. Pour into soup tureen, garnish with chopped parsley, and serve very hot.

IRISH BEEF BROTH

Beef broth kept the life in us during the January and February lambing season. At about nine o'clock these cold nights we had to go up the field to look after the sheep. If there were any newly-born lambs we had to bring them and their mothers back to the shed—not an easy task. We'd come home, cold and hungry, to a cheerful kitchen and a piping hot bowl of broth.

Ingredients: Serves: 8

1 lb boiling beef	**500 g**	
4 pints cold water	**2.5 litre**	10 cups
salt and pepper		
2 oz pearl barley	**50 g**	$\frac{1}{2}$ cup
1 lb diced mixed vegetables		
(onions, carrots, celery, white		
turnips)	**500 g**	4 cups
1 oz oatmeal	**25 g**	$\frac{1}{4}$ cup
bouquet garni		

Preparation time: 25 minutes   **Cooking time:** $2\frac{1}{2}$–3 hours

Method:
1. Remove excess fat from meat.
2. Put all ingredients into a saucepan, bring to the boil, cover and simmer.
3. Remove meat and bouquet garni.
4. Dice meat finely and return it to broth.
5. Bring to the boil and serve hot.

LAMB KIDNEY SOUP

Lamb kidneys are soft and strong in flavour and are often used in mixed grills.

Ingredients: Serves: 4

3 or 4 lamb's kidney		
1 larged diced onion		
4 oz diced turnip	**100 g**	1 cup
1 sliced potato		
$1\frac{1}{2}$ oz butter or margarine	**40 g**	2 tbsp.
1 oz flour	**25 g**	$\frac{1}{4}$ cup
$1\frac{3}{4}$ pints stock	**1 litre**	$4\frac{1}{2}$ cups
bouquet garni		
seasoning		

Preparation time: 20 minutes   **Cooking time:** $1\frac{1}{2}$ hours

Method:
1. Remove the membrane, fat and nerves from the kidney; steep in salted tepid water for 15 minutes, rinse a few times in cold

water.
2. Melt butter or margarine, brown the kidneys, add vegetables and cook for 1 or 2 minutes.
3. Add flour and mix well together, gradually add stock and bring to the boil.
4. Add bouquet garni and season to taste; cover and simmer for 1½ hours. Remove bouquet garni.

5. Liquidize soup or put through a sieve; reheat and check seasoning. Pour into soup tureen.

To vary:
Use a good bone stock, omitting margarine and flour. Bring soup to the boil, cover and transfer to the oven. Cook for the same length of time.

CHICKEN SOUP

At home, summer Saturday nights were special to us. Mother would cook chickens for a cold Sunday lunch, boiling two of them in a big pot with water, fresh vegetables and herbs. In the evening we'd come in from playing in the fields with plenty of appetite and sit down to big bowls full of chicken soup—really chicken stock but with a rich flavour—and dip slices of white bread into the soup as we ate.

Ingredients: Serves: 4

½ oz margarine or butter	15 g	¾ tbsp.
1 finely chopped onion		
1 oz flour	25 g	¼ cup
1¾ pints chicken stock	1 litre	4½ cups
seasoning		
8 oz sliced cooked chicken	225 g	1 cup
bouquet garni		
finely chopped parsley		

Preparation time: 15 minutes   **Cooking time:** 20 minutes

Method:

1. Melt margarine or butter and fry onion lightly without burning; add in flour and mix well together. Gradually add stock, bring to the boil and season to taste.
2. Add diced chicken and bouquet garni, bring back to the boil, cover and simmer for 20 minutes.

3. Remove bouquet garni, check seasoning.
4. Pour into soup tureen and garnish with chopped parsley.

To vary:
Omit margarine and flour, and instead add a few diced potatoes to the remaining ingredients. Cook for the same length of time.

If the oven is turned on, to save fuel prepare this soup in an ovenproof container. Bring it to the boil on burner top, cover and place in centre of oven for the twenty minutes' cooking time.

CABBAGE SOUP WITH BACON

In the not so long-ago days, cabbage was much in use among the Irish. Both cabbage and bacon were normally cooked in the same liquid and there was far less bacon than cabbage in the soup. Cabbage, bacon and potatoes were often cooked together and served as the main meal.

Ingredients: Serves: 4

1 oz butter or margarine	**25 g**	1½ tbsp.
8 oz finely chopped lean bacon	**225 g**	1⅓ cups
2 finely chopped onions		
2 oz thinly sliced mushrooms (reserve stalks and skins from mushrooms)	**50 g**	⅓ cup
5–6 cloves		
small head cabbage (stalks removed and finely shredded)		
3 diced potatoes		
1¾ pints vegetable stock	**1 litre**	5 cups
black pepper		

Preparation time: 15 minutes   **Cooking time:** 30–35 minutes

Method:

1. Melt butter or margarine in saucepan.
2. Add bacon, onion and sliced mushrooms; fry for a minute, stirring continuously.
3. Add the cabbage, potatoes, black pepper and stock.
4. Put mushroom stalks and skins along with cloves into a piece of muslin and tie up neatly, add to soup.
5. Bring to the boil, cover and simmer until all the vegetables are tender: for about 30 minutes.
6. Serve piping hot.

To economize:

Leftover cooked bacon may be diced and used instead of fresh bacon. Put this bacon into the soup ten minutes before cooking time is completed, bring back to boiling point, then simmer for 10 minutes.

GARDEN GREEN PEA SOUP

During the summer months we always picked peas before they had gone tough and stringy. The flavour of peas fresh from the field was far superior to those bought in any shop. It was a shock, though, when we were children and had picked, say six pounds of peas, to learn that by the time they were podded there were only enough for eight people.

It is best to cook fresh peas for about ten minutes in fast boiling water, strain them and then bury them in melted butter.

Ingredients: Serves: 4

2 oz butter	**50 g**	¼ cup
2 lb young garden peas	**1 kg**	5 cups
1 medium-sized diced cucumber		
3 finely chopped spring onions		
1 oz sugar	**25 g**	1½ tbsp.
finely chopped mint		
1¾ pints vegetable stock	**1 litre**	5 cups
salt and pepper		
a little cream		

Preparation time: 20 minutes   **Cooking time:** 10 minutes

Method:

1. Melt butter in a saucepan.
2. Fry vegetables in the butter.
3. Add sugar, mint and stock, bring to the boil and season to taste.
4. Simmer approximately 10 minutes until tender.
5. Liquidize soup or put through a sieve.
6. Bring back to the boil and serve immediately with a little cream poured over the top.

Watchpoints:

Pea soup is best made when the peas are young and fresh from the garden. The thin light green pods can be cooked as they are, and the soup then sieved to remove fibres. If the peas are old, remove the shucks before adding the peas to the soup.

CREAM OF VEGETABLE SOUP

Vegetable soup was the first soup most of us were introduced to as children. The foundation of a soup was the stock. We knew this, yet even more of us who loved cooking disliked hearing about rules for stockmaking. It took us time to realize that to make good soup we needed a good stock. October was the time of year for making stock—a cold and windy month when there were plenty of carrots, onions, turnips and tomatoes stored away for the winter season.

Ingredients: Serves: 4

1 lb mixed vegetables (chopped carrots, onions, white turnips, peas, tomatoes)	**500 g**	4 cups

2 oz butter or margarine	**50 g**	¼ cup
1 oz flour	**25 g**	1½ tbsp.
1¾ pints vegetable stock	**1 litre**	5 cups
seasoning		
4–5 tablespoons cream		

Preparation time: 15 minutes   **Cooking time:** 1½ hours

Method:

1. Melt butter or margarine in a saucepan, add vegetables and fry for two or three minutes. Remove from heat; stir in the flour.
2. Gradually add stock, bring to the boil and season well.
3. Cover and simmer for 1½ hours.
4. Liquidize soup or put it through a sieve.
5. Put back into the saucepan bring to the boil; check seasoning.
6. Pour into soup tureen and add cream.

To vary:

Use any vegetables that are in season. To add distinctive flavour add a crushed clove of garlic or a chopped green or red pepper. If flour is omitted add two or three extra diced potatoes. A quantity of milk can be substituted for a quantity of stock.

COLD SPINACH CREAM SOUP

In Ireland there are two main kinds of spinach. Summer spinach is light in colour and more delicate in flavour. The darker-coloured winter spinach requires a slightly longer cooking time.

Ingredients: Serves: 4–6

1 lb chopped cooked spinach	**500 g**	4 cups
½ pint sour cream or plain yogurt	**275 ml**	1¼ cups
1 pint spinach stock	**575 ml**	2½ cups
2 tablespoons lemon juice		
nutmeg		
seasoning		
thin slices of lemon (to serve)		

Preparation time: 15 minutes

Method:

1. Blend all ingredients together in liquidizer and season to taste.
2. Pour into soup tureen and serve with lemon slices.

To vary:

Substitute cucumber or lettuce for spinach.

Watchpoint:

Cooking spinach reduces its size to about half. Cold spinach soup should be chilled for about an hour before serving.

49

Fish

STUFFED OYSTERS

Centuries ago oysters were used in Ireland as a garnish or stuffing for practically any dish. Today they are very popular eaten raw—sometimes as "garnish" for a smooth pint of Guinness. Or they can be enjoyed in sauces or soups—or as a stuffing mixture as in this recipe.

Ingredients: Serves: 4

24 oysters		
1 oz butter or margarine	**25 g**	1½ tbsp.
1 finely chopped onion		
2 oz breadcrumbs	**50 g**	1 cup
1 crushed garlic clove		
3–4 tomatoes (skins removed and seeded)		
1 teaspoon finely chopped parsley		
a little milk		
seasoning		
3 oz grated cheddar cheese	**75 g**	¾ cup
lemon wedges		

Preparation time: 20 minutes   **Cooking time:** 10 minutes

Method:

1. Scrub oyster shells well, put into a saucepan over a moderate heat until shells open; reserve the liquid.
2. Remove flesh from the oyster shells and chop the oyster meat.
3. Heat the butter or margarine in a saucepan and fry onion and breadcrumbs for a minute.
4. Add crushed garlic, tomatoes and parsley.
5. Make up to ½ pint liquid, combining liquid from oysters with milk. Add to the saucepan with oyster meat.
6. Bring to the boil and heat through for 2 or 3 minutes, season to taste.

SKIBBEREEN EAGLES

Skibbereen eagles are scallops cooked in a wine sauce. Skibbereen is a town in west Cork, a region where some of our finest scallops are harvested. The newspaper there is *The Skibbereen Eagle*, famous in the past for objecting editorially to the misbehaviour of distant potentates like the Kaiser and the Tsar. Scallops are nearly as proud a product of the south Irish coast as this newspaper; the wine is what makes them fly.

Ingredients:

Serves: 4

8 scallops (save the shells)		
½ pint white wine	**275 ml**	1¼ cups
2 oz butter or margarine	**50 g**	¼ cup
8 oz sliced mushrooms	**225 g**	1½ cups
1 oz flour	**25 g**	¼ cup
4 oz garden peas	**100 g**	⅔ cup
salt and black pepper		
1 lb boiled potatoes, mashed and creamed	**500 g**	2 cups
sieved hard-boiled egg yolk		
finely chopped parsley		

Preparation time: 20 minutes   **Cooking time:** 18 minutes

Method:

1. Wash scallops and leave in cold fresh water for a few minutes.
2. Put scallops and wine into a saucepan and simmer for 4 to 5 minutes. Strain off and reserve liquid.
3. Remove flesh from scallop shells and cut each piece of flesh into four.
4. Melt the butter or margarine and lightly fry the mushrooms; add flour and cook for a further minute.
5. Gradually add the liquid, then add peas and bring to the boil; season to taste. Cover and simmer for 7 minutes until the peas are tender.
6. Add the scallop flesh and heat for 3 or 4 minutes.
7. Divide filling evenly among shells. Pipe potatoes on top of filling.
8. Set under the grill until nicely brown.
9. Serve immediately garnished with sieved egg yolk and parsley.

Watchpoint:

When using fresh oysters, make sure they're alive when you buy them; the shells should be closed.

BEDDED PRAWNS

Fresh shrimp may not be available, but frozen shelled cooked shrimp of good quality are always available, shrimps are not unlike tiny Dublin Bay prawns, with a soft outer shell and rounded backs, and with the tail tucked under the body.

Ingredients:

1 lb raw shrimps	**500 g**	2 cups
2 oz butter or margarine	**50 g**	¼ cup
4 oz finely chopped onion	**100 g**	1 cup
4 oz sliced mushrooms	**100 g**	¾ cup

1 oz flour	**25 g**	¼ cup
½ pint fish stock	**275 ml**	1¼ cups
1 tablespoon tomato purée		
seasoning		
2-3 tablespoons cream		
8 oz cooked long-grained rice	**225 g**	4 cups
cayenne pepper		

Preparation time: 20 minutes   **Cooking time:** 10–12 minutes

Method:

1. Cook shrimps in boiling salted water for 4 or 5 minutes. Drain, reserving the liquid, cool and shell the shrimps.
2. Melt the margarine or butter, add onion and mushrooms and cook 1 or 2 minutes until soft.
3. Add flour and cook for a minute.
4. Gradually add the liquid, bring to the boil and season to taste.
5. Add shrimps, tomato purée, and bring back to the boil; heat through for 1 or 2 minutes.
6. Arrange rice in an oval-shaped dish. Pile shrimp and vegetable sauce on top; sprinkle lightly with cayenne pepper.

To vary:
Use mashed potatoes instead of rice.

Watchpoint:
If frozen shrimpmeat is used, allow it to thaw before preparing.

PRAWN LUNCH

Dublin Bay prawns are a famous and popular shellfish, served in most Irish restaurants and hotels. When these shrimp for that is what they look like (only larger) are coated in batter and deep-fried we call the dish scampi. This recipe however places the shrimp in a thick savoury sauce in steaming hot potato cases.

Ingredients: Serves: 4

4 large potatoes		
1 oz butter or margarine	**25 g**	1½ tbsp.
1 seeded and finely chopped green pepper		
1 finely chopped onion		
1 oz flour	**25 g**	¼ cup
½ pint milk	**275 ml**	1¼ cups
8 oz cooked prawns	**225 g**	1 cup
salt and pepper		
paprika		

Preparation time: 20 minutes   **Cooking time:** 1 hour
Oven position: top   **Oven temperature:** gas 6, 200°C, 400°F

Method:

1. Scrub the potatoes and rinse under a cold tap. Dry and rub all over with a little butter or margarine.
2. Cut a cross in the top of each potato, put them all on a baking sheet and place in oven for 50 to 60 minutes.
3. Meantime heat the butter or margarine, add vegetables and cook for 2 or 3 minutes without browning.
4. Add flour and cook for a further minute. Gradually add the liquid, bring to the boil.
5. Scoop out the potato pulp carefully to avoid breaking shell, and keep hot.
6. Add the potato pulp and prawns to the sauce, bring to the boil, heat through for 2 or 3 minutes, check seasoning.
7. Divide filling evenly among potato cases, garnish with paprika, and serve piping hot.

DRESSED CRAWFISH

The flesh of this fish is very good. It is very like the lobster's but not quite as tender.

Ingredients: Serves: 2–3

1 crawfish		
1½ oz butter	**40 g**	2 tbsp.
¼ pint brandy	**150 ml**	½ cup
¼ pint cream	**150 ml**	½ cup
2 egg yolks		
8 oz long-grained boiled rice	**250 g**	4 cups

Preparation time: 25 minutes   **Cooking time:** 20 minutes

Method:

1. Plunge the crawfish into boiling salted water and cook for 20 to 30 minutes.
2. Remove the flesh from the body of the crawfish and cut into slices.
3. Heat the butter and add the flesh.
4. Heat brandy and pour over the fish and ignite with a match, then simmer for 3 or 4 minutes.
5. Blend the egg yolk with the cream, add to the fish, heat gently for a minute and place in a deep casserole.
6. Serve hot with boiled rice.

To economize:
Use a white stewing sauce in place of the combined brandy, cream and eggs.

CREAMED LOBSTER

Lobsters are increasingly scarce in Ireland because of foreign demand for them. When available they can be bought all year round; they are best, however, during the summer months. They live on the sea bed completely enclosed in their jointed shells. They are a blue-black colour and turn bright red when cooked. The female obster is tenderer and of a more delicate flavour than the male.

Ingredients: Serves: 2

1 lobster
½ pint mayonnaise   **250 ml**   1 cup
3-4 tablespoons cream
sliced radishes
tomatoes, chives
hard-boiled eggs
cucumber
paprika
finely chopped parsley

Preparation time: 35 minutes   **Cooking time:** 10-15 minutes

Watchpoint:

Lobster should always be bought live and may be killed by any of the following methods.

1. Cover the lobster with cold water and bring gradually to the boil; then cook for 10 to 15 minutes to the pound. Some think this the most humane method.
2. Plunge the live lobster into fast-boiling water for a few minutes. This kills it instantly.
3. Pierce the brain by putting a sharp knife or needle right through the cross on the head—also bringing instant death—and put immediately into boiling water.

Method:

1. Allow the cooked lobster to cool. Remove the flesh from claws and tail, reserving the shell.
2. Arrange the leaves of lettuce on a long dish or platter. Arrange the shell of lobster on top.
3. Fill the head shell with the claw meat. Arrange tail meat on its tail shells.
4. Mix the mayonnaise and cream together. Coat the lobster meat lightly with mayonnaise (serve the remainder in a sauce-boat).
5. Sprinkle paprika lightly over the mayonnaise.
6. Garnish dish with vegetables and sliced eggs.

ISLAND TREASURE

Crab can bring back happy memories to those who have gone hunting for them—on one of the Aran Islands off the west coast of Galway or on Achill off Mayo or Tory Island off the coast of Donegal. Among the larger shellfish crab is the one most widely available in Ireland.

Ingredients: Serves: 2-3

1 lb crab meat	**500 g**	2 cups
1 oz butter or margarine	**25 g**	1½ tbsp.

1 oz flour	**25 g**	¼ cup
½ pint milk	**275 ml**	1¼ cups

1 tablespoon lemon juice
1 tablespoon mustard
salt and freshly ground black pepper
cottage potatoes (to serve)

Preparation time: 15 minutes   **Cooking time:** 8 minutes

Method:

1. Melt the butter or margarine, add flour and cook for a minute. Gradually add milk, stirring continually.
2. Add lemon juice, mustard and crab meat. Bring to the boil and season to taste.
3. Cook for 3 or 4 minutes.
4. Serve hot with cottage potatoes.

BLACK SOLE ON THE BONE

The best of the three main varieties of sole—black, lemon and megrim (or white)—is the black or slip or Dover sole, whose flavour is perhaps the finest found in any flat fish.

Ingredients: Serves: 1

1 medium-sized fillet of black sole
a little cooking oil
salt and pepper
lemon juice
lemon wedges
chopped parsley

Preparation time: 5 minutes   **Cooking time:** 10 minutes

Method:

1. Preheat grill.
2. Brush the sole with cooking oil and sprinkle with salt and pepper. Add lemon juice.
3. Put on to grill and cook for 5 minutes on each side.
4. Set out on a serving dish; garnish with lemon wedges and chopped parsley.

Watchpoint:
Small fish are best cooked on the bone.

SOLE ROLL

Lemon sole, which is in season in Ireland from July to February, is a delicate milky fish.

Ingredients: Serves: 4

4 fillets lemon sole	
juice and rind of 1 lemon	
1 tablespoon flour	**25 g**

55

2 bananas
1 oz butter or margarine   **25 g**   1½ tbsp.
1 banana sliced and dipped in
   lemon juice

Preparation time: 15 minutes   **Cooking time:** 20 minutes
Oven position: centre   **Oven temperature:**
   gas 6, 200°C, 400°F

Method:

1. Trim the fillets.
2. Mix lemon rind with flour.
3. Cut bananas in two (on the width). Dip into lemon juice and dip in flour mixture.
4. Lay each banana piece on a fillet and roll fillet around banana.
5. Place in casserole dish and dot with butter.
6. Serve sole on preheated serving dish; garnish with banana slices.

SEACAKES

The flesh of ray is very delicate and is a good choice for this dish. But any seafish may be used.

Ingredients: Serves: 4

8 oz cooked ray   **255 g**   1 cup
1 finely chopped onion
1 teaspoon finely chopped parsley
8 oz mashed potatoes   **255 g**   1 cup
seasoning
1 tablespoon tomato ketchup
1 egg
4 oz breadcrumbs   **100 g**   2 cups
2 tablespoons cooking oil
lemon wedges

Preparation time: 15 minutes   **Cooking time:** 15 minutes

Method:

1. Flake the fish and put into a bowl; add onion, parsley and potatoes; bind well together and season to taste, moistening with tomato ketchup.
2. Form into 8 balls; flatten them into round shapes.
3. Brush them over with beaten egg and dip in breadcrumbs.
4. Heat the oil; then fry fish cakes in it until they are golden brown.
5. Arrange on serving dish and garnish with lemon wedges.

Watchpoint:

To get a nicer appearance, sieve the breadcrumbs once or twice before using.

FRIED PLAICE

Tradition has it that Moses once began cooking a flat fish, and when the fish was half-cooked his fire went out. In a fit of temper Moses threw the fish into the water and the fish came to life again. And so ever since then all flat fish have remained white on one side and dark on the other.

Plaice, as mentioned earlier, is our most popular flat fish, and is in season all year round. But any flat or white fish may be substituted in this recipe.

Ingredients: Serves: 1

1 medium-sized plaice
1 tablespoon well-seasoned flour
a little milk
fine breadcrumbs
cooking oil
lemon wedges
1 oz butter   **25 g**   1½ tbsp.

Preparation time: 5 minutes   **Cooking time:** 8–10 minutes

Method:
1. Remove fins and gut the fish, leaving head on. Wash well.
2. Dip in seasoned flour.
3. Dip fish in milk and coat in breadcrumbs.
4. Heat the oil; fry the fish over a gentle heat, allowing 4 or 5 minutes for each side.
5. Chop parsley very fine and beat this into a large knob of butter.
6. Serve fish hot, and garnished with the parsley butter and lemon slices.

POACHED TURBOT

Turbot is a gamier sort of fish, which is why it is sometimes called the pheasant of the sea. In season all year round in Ireland, it is at its best from March to September.

Ingredients: Serves: 1–2

1 small turbot
1 pint water   **575 ml**   2½ cups
½ pint dry white wine   **275 ml**   1¼ cups
1–2 tablespoons white wine vinegar
2 cleaned and sliced carrots
2 finely chopped onions
16 black peppercorns
bouquet garni
4 oz butter   **100 g**   ½ cup
grated horseradish
1 teaspoon finely chopped parsley

lemon wedges

Preparation time: 35 minutes   **Cooking time:** 45 minutes

Method:

1. Remove fins and gut the turbot. Wash well. Season it and leave for 30 minutes.
2. Meantime put water, white wine vinegar, carrots, onions, peppercorns and bouquet garni into a saucepan and simmer for 30 minutes. Allow to cool.
3. Put in the fish; bring slowly to the boil over a gentle heat; simmer for 15 minutes.
4. Melt butter, and add to it horseradish and parsley.
5. Put the horseradish butter in a sauce boat.
6. Serve the strained turbot on a preheated serving plate garnished with lemon wedges.

FARMHOUSE FISH STEW

Brill is in season all year but in Ireland it is at its best in early spring. This stew is very good with brill, but any fresh river fish would suit the recipe.

Ingredients: Serves: 4

1 lb brill fillet	**500 g**	2 cups
2 oz flour	**50 g**	½ cup
seasoning		
3 tablespoons cooking oil		
1 thinly sliced onion		
1 seeded and chopped green pepper		
1 teaspoon curry powder		
a large pinch of ground ginger		
6 tomatoes (skinned, seeded and chopped)		
1 tablespoon chutney		
½ pint fish stock	**275 ml**	1¼ cups
8 oz long-grained rice	**225 g**	1 cup

Preparation time: 20 minutes   **Cooking time:** 10 minutes
Oven position: centre   **Oven temperature:**
gas 6, 200°C, 400°F

Method:

1. Wipe the fish, remove the skin and bones, then cut into chunks.
2. Season the flour with salt and pepper; coat the fish in seasoned flour (reserve leftover flour).
3. Heat 2 tablespoons oil in a casserole and fry the fish until it is beginning to brown, then remove.
4. Heat remaining oil, add onion and pepper, cook until soft; stir in the remaining flour, curry powder, ground ginger, tomatoes and chutney, gradually add the stock, stirring continuously until the sauce thickens. Add

58

the fish, bring to the boil; check seasoning.
5. Put the lid on the casserole and place in the oven for 20 minutes.
6. Meantime put the rice into a casserole; add twice as much water as rice to the rice and one teaspoon of salt. Place in the centre of oven without covering for 20 minutes.

7. Spoon the fish mixture into the centre of preheated serving plate.

Watchpoint:
The flesh of brill should be firm and slightly creamy. A bluish tinge denotes staleness.

COD IN A QUILT

Cod was always a popular fish in Ireland: good, plentiful and relatively inexpensive. It was often served for Friday lunch, generally with a plain white sauce and fresh vegetables. Today Irish cooks are more venturesome and cod is often prepared in more exotic ways. Here is a soufflé dish.

Ingredients: Serves: 4

soufflé dish:		
1 oz margarine	**25 g**	1½ tbsp.
fine breadcrumbs		
filling:		
1 oz butter	**25 g**	1½ tbsp.
1 oz flour	**25 g**	¼ cup
½ pint milk	**275 ml**	1¼ cups
seasoning		
4 egg yolks		
5 egg whites		
8 oz cooked cod	**225 g**	1 cup

Preparation time: 20 minutes   **Cooking time:** 35–40 minutes
Oven position: centre   **Oven temperature:**
gas 5, 190°C, 375°F

Method for preparing souffle dish: 1½ pint (3 cups)

1. Prepare soufflé case by greasing with melted margarine and dust with breadcrumbs.
2. Cut out a double sheet of brown or greaseproof paper 1½ times the depth of soufflé case allowing an inch on the width to overlap.
3. Tie this strip around the outer edge of soufflé dish and grease the paper well.

Method for preparing filling:
1. Melt butter or margarine and remove from the heat; add flour and beat well together.
2. Add the milk and stir until it just reaches boiling point; season to taste and allow to cool.
3. Beat the yolks one at a time into the same mixture. Allow to

59

cool.

4. Beat the egg whites with egg beater until firm. Add a tablespoon to the mixture to soften, then quickly fold in remainder.

5. Put half the mixture into prepared soufflé dish, top with flaked cod, then add the rest of the mixture.

6. Place in the oven and bake.

COD CREAMY PIE

Often on Thursday evenings during the summer months we would go to Kilmore Quay, a village in South Wexford and one of the principal Irish whitefish ports, to get a supply of cod for Friday's lunch.

Cod is a bland fish. So it is best served with a highly seasoned sauce, as in this recipe.

Ingredients: Serves: 4

4 oz peas	**100 g**	⅔ cup
1 lb cooked cod	**500 g**	2 cups
1 oz cornflour (cornstarch)	**25 g**	2 tbsp.
½ pint milk	**275 ml**	1¼ cups
½ pint fish stock	**275 ml**	1¼ cups
3–4 sliced tomatoes		
3–4 medium-sized sliced and cooked potatoes		
seasoning		
3 oz grated cheese	**75 g**	¾ cup

Preparation time: 15 minutes   **Cooking time:** 25 minutes
Oven position: centre   **Oven temperature:**
gas 4, 180°C, 350°F

Method:

1. Cook peas in boiling salted water for 5 minutes.
2. Flake fish; put half into the bottom of an ovenproof casserole.
3. Blend the cornstarch with a little milk, and set aside.
4. Put the remaining milk and the fish stock in a saucepan and bring to the boil; add blended cornstarch, stirring continuously.
5. Layer the fish and vegetables in a casserole and season to taste.
6. Pour the sauce over the contents of the casserole.
7. Sprinkle with grated cheese and bake for 25 minutes.

BAKED HAKE

Some Irish regard hake as the *filet mignon* of the cod family. It makes a lovely oven dish.

Ingredients: Serves: 4

1 lb hake fillets	**500 g**	2 cups

2 finely chopped onions
3 tomatoes (skinned, seeded and
   quartered)
salt and pepper

½ pint fish stock	**275 ml**	1¼ cups
2 oz grated cheese	**50 g**	½ cup
1 lb hot mashed potatoes	**500 g**	2 cups

Preparation time: 20 minutes   **Cooking time:** 25–30 minutes
Oven position: centre   **Oven temperature:**
                                                              gas 5, 190°C, 375°F

Method:
1. Place hake fillets in a greased ovenproof dish.
2. Sprinkle onions on top of fish, add tomatoes and stock, season to taste; cover and put into the oven for 25 to 30 minutes.
3. When baked, pipe potatoes around the edge of dish, sprinkle fish with cheese and put under a hot grill or back into the hot oven to brown.
4. Serve hot.

BUTTERED WHITING

Whiting, sometimes called the chicken of the sea, is best from May to January though in season all year round. It is a delicately flavoured fish, very easily digested.

Ingredients: Serves: 4

4 fillets whiting
2 lemons
wine sauce:
1 glass white wine
1 finely chopped shallot
6 peppercorns
1 egg yolk

2 oz butter	**50 g**	¼ cup
white sauce		
1 oz butter or margarine	**25 g**	1½ tbsp.
1 oz flour	**25 g**	2 tbsp.
½ pint fish stock	**275 ml**	1¼ cups

seasoning
wedges of lemon
chopped parsley

Preparation time: 20 minutes   **Cooking time:** 20 minutes
Oven position: top   **Oven temperature:** gas 6, 200°C, 400°F

Method for fish:
1. Skin the fillets, wash and dry.

Prepare stock from bones and

skin.

2. Fold fillets and place in buttered dish, sprinkle with lemon juice and add 2 or 3 tablespoons of fish stock.

3. Cover with buttered greaseproof paper.

Method for wine sauce:

1. Put wine into a saucepan with shallot and peppercorns. Reduce over a fast heat to one dessertspoonful.

2. Put yolk into bowl and beat reduced wine into it.

3. Place bowl over a saucepan of warm water, adding the butter bit by bit and beating continuously.

Method for white sauce:

1. Melt the fat, add the flour and cook to a pale straw colour for a minute or so.

2. Add the stock and stir with wooden spoon until boiling.

3. Season and beat in the wine sauce.

To serve:

Arrange fillets in the centre of dish and coat with sauce. Garnish with lemon wedges and chopped parsley.

To economize and vary:

Omit the wine sauce. Add some cooked vegetables to the white sauce, bring to the boil, heat through for a few minutes and pour over the fish.

FISH BOATS

Great quantities of haddock are landed all around the coast of Ireland. One of our principal fishing ports for haddock as well as cod and whiting is at Howth, just above Dublin. Haddock is recognized by the black thumbprint on the shoulder, which legend tells us is supposed to represent the mark of the finger and thumb of St Peter when he drew the fish out of the lake of Gennesaret.

Ingredients: Serves: 4

6 oz shortcrust pastry	**175 g**	1½ cups
filling:		
6 oz cooked haddock	**175 g**	1½ cups
1 oz butter or margarine	**25 g**	1½ tbsp.
1 oz flour	**25 g**	2 tbsp.
½ pint milk	**275 ml**	1¼ cups
2 oz cooked peas	**50 g**	⅓ cup
seasoning		
finely chopped parsley		

finely chopped parsley

Preparation time: 20 minutes   **Cooking time:** 15–20 minutes
Oven position: centre   **Oven temperature:**
                                                    gas 6, 200°C, 400°F

Method for pastry:

1. Make basic shortcrust pastry.
2. Turn pastry onto a floured board, knead, roll out and line 12 muffin tins; cover each tartlet with a piece of brown paper and place some rice or macaroni on top for weight.
3. Put into the oven and bake for 15 to 20 minutes.

Method for filling:

1. Flake the fish.
2. Melt butter or margarine, remove from the heat, add flour and mix together. Add the milk and bring to the boil.

3. Add haddock and cooked peas; season to taste and bring to the boil.
4. Set the tartlets out on a serving dish and divide the mixture among them. Serve hot or cold, sprinkled with finely chopped parsley.

To vary:

Roll out pastry and line an 8-inch cake tin with it. Use other fish and vegetables that may be fresher and available.

SMOKED HADDOCK

Long ago fish had to be smoked to preserve it. Today fish is salted and smoked to give it an attractive appearance and distinctive flavour. When split, gutted, cured and smoked with the back bone left in, the haddock is sold as Finnan Haddock.

Ingredients: Serves: 4

pastry:		
6 oz plain flour	**175 g**	1½ cups
pinch of salt		
4 oz butter or margarine	**100 g**	½ cup
1 oz shortening	**25 g**	1½ tbsp.
1 egg yolk		
1–2 tablespoons water		
filling:		
1 lb cooked smoked haddock	**500 g**	2 cups
1 small bunch of spring onions		
2 quartered hard-boiled eggs		
sauce:		
1 oz butter	**25g**	1½ tbsp.
¾ oz flour		1½ tbsp.
¼ pint milk	**150 ml**	⅝ cup
garnish:		
1 lb potato purée mixed with an egg yolk	**500 g**	2 cups
2 oz grated cheese	**50 g**	½ cup

Preparation time: 25 minutes   **Cooking time:** 25 minutes
Oven position: top   **Oven temperature:** gas 6, 200°C, 400°F

Method for pastry:

1. Sieve flour and salt into a bowl, cut butter or margarine into it until well coated with the flour. Using finger tips, rub the butter or margarine into the flour until the mixture resembles fine breadcrumbs.
2. Mix egg yolk and water together; add this to the buttered flour and mix to a firm dough.
3. Turn onto a floured board; knead lightly until smooth.
4. Line a 9-inch pie pan with the pastry. Bake for 25 minutes unfilled by covering base of pastry with greaseproof or brown paper and placing some rice or macaroni on top for weight.
5. Remove rice and paper and place pastry shell on serving plate.

Method for filling:

1. Flake fish.
2. Blanch the spring onions by putting into cold water and bringing to the boil. Drain off water.
3. Place the fish at the bottom of the pastry shell; put the onions over, and the quartered eggs around.

Method for sauce:

1. Melt butter or margarine, add the flour and cook for 1 minute.
2. Gradually add the milk and bring to the boil, stirring all the time.

Method for garnishing:

1. Spoon sauce over the onions and eggs.
2. Pipe potato purée across the top in lattice fashion.
3. Sprinkle with grated cheese and brown in a hot oven.

To vary:

Omit egg yolk from pastry and add additional water as a binder. Use other fish and vegetables that are fresh and available.

SALMON STEAK

Salmon are the leaping kings of sea and river, and take from two to seven years to mature. Salmon spend most of their lives in the ocean; they return to rivers like the Fee in Galway or the Moy in Mayo to spawn. They're caught in the spawning season sometimes in an estuary just as they're leaving the sea. When fresh from the river, salmon are a lovely light orange colour and have a beautiful flavour.

Ingredients: Serves: 4

4 salmon steaks
black pepper
4 tablespoons finely chopped
    shallots
rind and juice of half lemon

½ pint white wine   **275 ml**   1¼ cups
4 oz seeded green grapes   **100 g**   1 cup
1 teaspoon cornflour blended
    in a tablespoon milk   2 tsp.
wedges of lemon

Preparation time: 15 minutes   Cooking time: 20 minutes
Oven position: centre   **Oven temperature:**
       gas 6, 200°C, 400°F

Method:

1. Arrange salmon in a buttered casserole dish and season with black pepper.
2. Add the shallots, rind, juice of lemon and wine.
3. Cover with a buttered sheet of greaseproof or brown paper and bake for 15 minutes.
4. Put grapes into the dish and cook for a further five minutes.
5. Set salmon on a serving dish; keep warm.
6. Pour blended cornflour into the dish; bring to the boil over a fast heat, stirring continuously; cook for a minute.
7. Spoon a little sauce over the salmon and garnish with lemon wedges.
8. Serve remaining sauce in sauceboat.

To economize and vary:

In place of white wine use a good stock.

TOMADILLY SAUCED TROUT

At home in Tomadilly we often ate trout, the river Slaney a few fields down was so plentifully stocked with them. When we were young we were allowed to watch the night fishing if we promised to sit quiet at the riverside and not frighten the fish.

Ingredients: **Serves: 4**

4 trout
juice of ½ lemon
seasoning
Sauce:
2 green or red peppers
4–5 tomatoes
1 tablespoon oil
1 chopped shallot or small onion
1 crushed clove of garlic
cayenne pepper
seasoning

Preparation time: 15 minutes   Cooking time: 20 minutes

Oven position: centre

Oven temperature:
gas 6, 200°C, 400°F

Method for trout:

1. Clean and bone the trout, wash and dry well.
2. Place in a greased ovenproof dish. Pour lemon juice over and season to taste. Cover with a greased sheet of greaseproof paper.

Method for sauce:

1. Blanch the peppers: put into cold water, bring to the boil and rinse under the cold tap.
2. Skin the tomatoes: put into a bowl and pour boiling water over them; leave for a minute, peel off skins, remove seeds and slice.

3. Heat the oil and add the shallot; cook until soft, then add tomatoes, crushed garlic, cayenne pepper and seasoning. Simmer to a rich pulp. Add the peppers and continue cooking for two or three minutes. Put through a sieve.
4. Arrange the trout on a serving dish and spoon the sauce over it.

Watchpoint:

It is helpful to leave the head on the fish while cooking. When the eyes turn white, the fish is cooked.

STUFFED MACKEREL

Mackerel is a tasty fish but heavy with a high fat content. It is lightened and complemented when stuffed with fruit: gooseberries, oranges or lemons.

Ingredients: Serves: 4

4 mackerel		
rind and juice of 1 orange		
stuffing:		
4 oz breadcrumbs	**100 g**	2 cups
1 teaspoon finely chopped parsley		
1 finely chopped shallot or small onion		
1 crushed clove of garlic		
seasoning		
1 oz butter	**25 g**	1½ tbsp.
orange slices		

Preparation time: 15 minutes
Oven position: centre

Cooking time: 20 minutes
Oven temperature:
gas 6, 200°C, 400°F

Method:

1. Clean and bone the mackerel; wash and dry well.
2. Put breadcrumbs, parsley, shallot, garlic, rind and orange juice into a bowl, mix well together, season to taste.
3. Divide this mixture evenly and stuff the 4 mackerel.

66

4. Place in greased ovenproof dish; dot with nuts of butter and bake for 20 minutes.

5. Arrange on serving dish and garnish with orange slices.

OATMEAL HERRING

This is a traditional Irish dish.

During the winter months herring used to be sold on the street in small Irish towns: a dozen herrings cost very little. The herring were gutted and washed, coated with milk and often with oatmeal before being put on to fry in a big heavy pan. After the harvest there was an abundant store of oatmeal, and some of this could be used to dress herring. Oatmeal had a nutty bite that complemented the taste of the herring.

Ingredients: Serves: 4

4 herrings		
salt		
$\frac{1}{4}$ pint milk	**150 ml**	$\frac{5}{8}$ cup
2 oz oatmeal	**50 g**	$\frac{1}{3}$ cup
2 oz butter or margarine	**50 g**	$\frac{1}{4}$ cup
finely chopped parsley		
lemon wedges		

Preparation time: 20 minutes   **Cooking time:** 15 minutes

Method:
1. Gut the herring, wash well in cold salted water, a .d dry.
2. Dip the herring in milk and roll well in oatmeal.
3. Heat the butter or margarine and, when the smoke is rising, fry the coated herring for 6 to 7 minutes on each side.
4. Garnish with parsley and lemon wedges, and serve hot.

WEIGHTS AND MEASURES

An important point to remember with regard to solid measures. Irish cooks are generous with their teaspoon and tablespoon measures: these are usually heaped, while the American cook levels off the quantity on the spoon with a knife. So it is important to note that where a recipe specifies a teaspoon of sugar, for example, you should use a rounded teaspoonful, i.e. as much above the spoon as in it, or **two** level teaspoonfuls.

Meat

IRISH LAMB - The main cuts

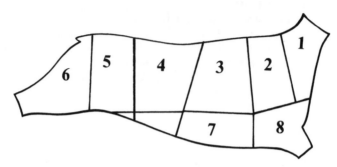

1. NECK
An inexpensive cut ideal for stews, casseroles and soups.

2. GIGOT *(chops)*
A medium-priced cut from the shoulder area ideal for casseroles and delicious in Irish stew.

3. FAIR END *(cutlets)*
A medium-priced cut sold as chops or cutlets which can be grilled or fried.

4. LOIN *(loin roast, saddle and chops)*
Expensive cuts. The chops can be grilled or fried. The loin can be roasted and the rib end of loin or rack—the saddle (or double loin cut)—is an ideal roast for special occasions.

5. FILLET *(roast)*
This is an expensive but succulent roasting joint from the top of the leg.

6. LEG *(roast)*
An expensive cut from the hind shank and excellent for roasting. Cuts from the lower shank are inexpensive and excellent for savoury casseroles.

7. BREAST *(with bone or boned and rolled)*
An inexpensive cut best for stewing or slow-roasting (a delicious roast when stuffed and rolled) and in casseroles.

8. SHOULDER *(roast and chops)*
Medium-priced cut which can be stuffed or even boned and rolled; chops cut are economical. Lamb shoulder is ideal for slow-roasting and braising.

LAMB SAUSAGES

Minced meat or mince—what Americans call hamburger—is a staple with Irish cooks because of its reasonable price. It may be bought already minced by the butcher, or bought as round steak and minced on the spot. Mince is versatile. It can be prepared in burger or meat loaf; it can be used in pies, tarts and casseroles, or as a stuffing for peppers and other vegetables.

Ingredients: Serves: 4–6

1 finely chopped onion		
1 lb lean minced lamb	**500 g**	2 cups
4 oz white breadcrumbs	**100 g**	2 cups
1 egg		
1 egg		
1 tablespoon chopped parsley		
1 teaspoon chopped mint		
pinch of oregano		
1 crushed clove of garlic		
seasoning		
1 tablespoon oil		
1 tablespoon wine vinegar		
1 tablespoon boiling water		
oil for shallow frying		

Preparation time: 15 minutes   **Cooking time:** 15–20 minutes

Method:

1. Combine all ingredients together and season to taste.
2. Flour hands and shape mixture into 16 sausage shapes; fry over a gentle heat for 20 minutes until golden brown.
3. Drain well and serve hot.

To vary:

Sausages can be coated with beaten egg and fine breadcrumbs, and then deep-fat fried until golden brown. Or mashed potatoes can be used instead of breadcrumbs.

STUFFED LAMB'S HEART

A heart requires basting during cooking, and is best with a highly seasoned and flavoured stuffing.

Ingredients: Serves: 4

1 lamb's heart		
1 apple		
1 oz butter or margarine	**25 g**	1½ tbsp.
1 finely chopped onion		
4 oz breadcrumbs	**100 g**	2 cups
1 teaspoon finely chopped herbs		

1 egg
2–3 tablespoons oil or 2 oz melted
   margarine   **50 g**   ¼ cup

Preparation time: 20 minutes   **Cooking time:** 1 hour
Oven position: centre   **Oven temperature:**
                                        gas 6, 200°C, 400°F

Method:

1. Wash the heart well in cold salted water, remove the valves. Put to steep in salted tepid water for 15 minutes, then wash under cold running tap.
2. In the meantime, make the stuffing, peel, core and chop the apple finely.
3. Melt the butter or margarine and fry the onion without browning, add the apple and continue cooking for a further minute.
4. Put the breadcrumbs and herbs into a bowl, add the onion and apple. Season to taste.
5. Bind with egg.
6. Dry the heart and cut between the internal tissue, fill the cavity with stuffing. Put into deep tin; pour oil over.
7. Cover and place in the oven for an hour, baste frequently during cooking.

To vary:

Serve hot sliced with a highly seasoned brown gravy or serve cold with a vegetable salad and salad dressing. Extra fruit and nuts may be added to the stuffing. Tinned fruit may be used and the fruit juice substituted for the egg to bind the stuffing.

IRISH STEW

There is a saying in the country that a stew boiled is a stew spoiled. Long slow cooking is of the essence of a good stew, bringing out the flavour of the mutton.

In this stew the meat is not browned first, but is put right in and cooked together with the onions and potatoes that give it its Irish temperament.

Ingredients: Serves: 4

2 lbs neck of mutton or
   4 shoulder chops   **1 kg**
1 lb potatoes   **500 g**   2 cups
6 medium onions
¾ pint cold water   **500 ml**   2 cups
seasoning
finely chopped parsley

Preparation time: 20 minutes   **Cooking time:** 2 hours

Method:

1. Remove any excess fat from the meat and cut it into neat pieces.

2. Wash and peel the potatoes. If small leave whole; if large, cut in two. Slice up one of them into thin pieces.
3. Peel the onions and chop one up.
4. Put the meat in the bottom of a heavy saucepan, then put in sliced potato, onion; season to taste, pour on water, bring to the boil, skim, cover and simmer for 1 hour.
5. Put in all other potatoes and onions, cover and simmer for a further hour.
6. Arrange meat in the centre of the serving dish with potatoes and onions arranged around it. Spoon a little sauce over. Serve remaining sauce in a sauceboat.
7. Garnish with parsley.

Watchpoint:

Gentle simmer is the key: keep the stew liquid "smiling"—i.e., just barely moving.

MIXED GRILL

Up until about ten years ago a mixed grill was usually the highlight of an Irish country family's day when they went up to Dublin or the larger towns. At six o'clock or so, after spending a long day out shopping, the country people would go to a hotel and order mixed grills. These were basically the same in all our hotels. There was usually a choice of puddings, tomatoes, egg, liver, kidney, rashers, sausages and chops, served with chips, plenty of soda bread, butter, jam and tea.

Ingredients:

1 kidney
1 slice of lamb's liver
1 loin lamb chop
1 back rasher
2 sausages
1 halved tomato
a little cooking oil
5–6 mushrooms
1 tablespoon butter
salt and pepper
finely chopped parsley
chipped potatoes

Serves: 1

Preparation time: 20 minutes

Cooking time: 15 minutes

Method:
1. Remove the membrane from the kidney, divide in 2 on the length, and remove the nerves.
2. Rinse the kidney along with the liver in tepid water a few times.
3. Put into salted tepid water for ten minutes, then rinse in cold water.
4. Brush lamb chops, kidney and liver with cooking oil, set on previously warmed grill with rasher.

71

5. Cook sausages until evenly browned on all sides, turn kidney, liver, rasher, and chop over onto other side; put on the tomato and mushrooms, put a knob of butter on top of each mushroom and season with salt and pepper. Grill for a further 5 to 7 minutes.

6. Arrange meats and vegetables on preheated plate.

7. Serve hot, garnished with parsley, with freshly fried chips.

CONNEMARA ROAST LAMB

Sheep reared on the mountain slopes of Connemara seem to have a distinctive juiciness and delicate flavour. Lean lamb, lower in calories than beef or pork, is an ideal meat for dieters. Lamb is best eaten hot.

Ingredients: Serves: 4–6

2½ lbs best end neck of lamb	1 kg	
½ oz melted butter	15 g	¾ tbsp.
1 glass red wine		
sauce:		
1 oz margarine	25 g	1½ tbsp.
1 finely chopped onion		
1 crushed clove garlic		
½ oz flour	15 g	1 tbsp.
¼ pint stock	150 ml	½ cup
1 glass red wine		
1 tablespoon tomato purée		
1 teaspoon chopped mixed herbs		
seasoning		
garnish:		
1 lb boiled potatoes	500 g	2 cups
1 oz melted butter	25 g	1½ tbsp.
finely chopped parsley		

Preparation time: 20 minutes
Oven position: centre

Cooking time: 1 hour
Oven temperature:
gas 6, 200°C, 400°F

Method:

1. Remove bones from meat and tie securely.
2. Put into roasting tin, dot with butter; pour glass of wine over.
3. Cook for an hour, basting well.

Method for sauce:

1. Melt the margarine, gently fry the onion, add garlic.
2. Add the flour; using a metal spoon, stir over a gentle heat till colour is golden brown.
3. Add stock, gradually add glass of wine, bring to the boil, add tomato purée; simmer for 5 or 6 minutes. Add herbs and check seasoning. Put through a sieve.

Method for serving meat:

1. Carve the meat and arrange

overlapping slices on one side of the dish.

2. Spoon a little sauce over the meat, pouring remainder into a sauceboat.
3. Arrange potatoes on other side of dish and pour a little melted butter over them.

4. Garnish with finely chopped parsley.

Watchpoints:

Lamb should be eaten fresh as it decomposes rapidly. Mutton is sheepmeat and not lamb; it should not be sold as lamb but often is.

MONDAY LUNCH

Monday lunches very often consist of meat left over from Sunday's roast. *"réchauffés"* the French call them: dressed up dishes made from pre-cooked meat. All sorts of cooked meats are used: lamb, mutton, beef, veal, pork, ham, poultry or game, but not in combination.

This is a meat casserole fixed the way my mother used to do it.

Ingredients: Serves: 4

1 lb cooked meat	500 g	2 cups
3 tablespoons oil		
2 finely chopped onions		
3–4 tomatoes (seeded, chopped and skinned)		
pinch of cinnamon		
1 oz flour	25 g	¼ cup
½ pint stock	275 ml	1¼ cups
4 oz cooked peas	100 g	2 cups
seasoning		
1 lb creamed potatoes	500 g	2 cups
4 oz cheddar cheese	100 g	1 cup
paprika		

Preparation time: 20 minutes   **Cooking time:** 15 minutes

Method:

1. Cut meat into one-inch squares.
2. Heat oil in a saucepan, fry onion for a minute over a gentle heat. Add tomatoes and cinnamon, continue cooking for a further minute.
3. Add flour and blend well with the vegetables.
4. Gradually add the stock, stirring continuously, add meat and peas, season to taste.

5. Bring just to boiling point and simmer for 10 to 12 minutes.
6. Pour the meat mixture in the centre of dish. Sprinkle with cheese and place under hot grill until golden brown.
7. Serve with potatoes piped around the edge of the dish and sprinkle with paprika.

73

Watchpoints:

If using a sauce in a reheated dish, the sauce should be slightly warmed before the meat is put in, then the entire contents slowly brought to boiling point. If meat is put into a boiling sauce, it will toughen. Use a white sauce for white meats and a brown sauce for brown meats. Always use a well flavoured and seasoned sauce. Garnish well. A good salad helps enhance the dish.

IRISH BEEF - The main cuts

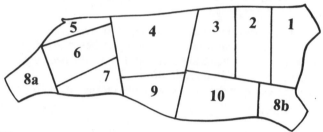

1. NECK
An inexpensive cut, best braised or stewed.

2. CHUCK *(blade roasts and Housekeeper's cut)*
Medium-priced cuts, best braised or stewed.

3. RIB ROAST *(back rib, fore rib, wing rib cuts)*
These cuts range from medium-priced to expensive but are suitable for roasting; meat can be boned from a rolled rib roast.

4. SIRLOIN *(roast and steak cuts)*
T-bone steaks, sirloin roast and sirloin steaks (from the fillet piece) are all expensive cuts. The sirloin can be roasted with the bone (a prime roasting joint) or it can be boned and rolled. The steaks can easily be grilled.

5. TAIL END
An inexpensive cut suitable for braising or stewing.

6. ROUND *(roast and steak cuts)*
Medium-priced cuts ideal for stewing or braising.

7. RUMP *(roast and steak cuts)*
Medium-priced to expensive cuts for braising, broiling or shallow frying.

8a & 8b. SHIN *(with bone or boned and cut into pieces)*
An inexpensive cut of lean meat which has some gristle. Ideal for slow stewing as it is very tasty. This cut can also be minced.

9. FLANK *(steak cuts or diced)*
A relatively inexpensive cut best for braising or stewing. It can also be minced.

10. BRISKET *(fresh or corned, boned and rolled)*

A good economical cut. Fresh brisket is ideal for pot roasting or braising. Corned brisket is suitable for corned beef and cabbage dishes.

HERE COMES EVERYBODY

This is a beefsteak and kidney pie—a great favourite in Irish homes: the sort of dish that ensures that everyone has a substantial meal. Essentially it is made by putting plenty of seasonal vegetables with meat and a lightly flavoured sauce into a baking tin or earthenware dish and covering them with a rich pastry.

Ingredients: Serves: 4–6

2 lbs round steak	**1 kg**		
8 oz ox or lamb's kidney	**225 g**	1 cup	
1 oz margarine	**25 g**	1½ tbsp.	
8 oz washed and sliced carrots	**225 g**	2 cups	
4 oz tomatoes (skinned, seeded and sliced)	**100 g**	⅔ cup	
2 peeled and sliced onions			
1 oz flour	**25 g**	¼ cup	
¾ pint stock	**425 ml**	1⅞ cups	
bouquet garni			
1 tablespoon tomato purée			
seasoning			
pastry:			
8 oz rough puff pastry	**225 g**	2 cups	
beaten egg yolk			
finely chopped parsley			

Preparation time: 30 minutes   **Cooking time:** 2 hours
Oven position: top   **Oven temperature:** gas 6, 200°C, 400°F

Method:

1. Remove any surplus fat from the meat, cutting the steak into one-inch cubes.
2. Remove membrane and nerves from the kidney, wash and cut into small pieces. Steep in tepid water for 15 minutes. Remove and rinse well in cold water.
3. Melt margarine and put in the steak and kidney and brown on all sides. Remove the meat and fry the vegetables; add flour and cook for one or two minutes.
4. Gradually add the stock, stirring continuously with a metal spoon.
5. Add the meat, bouquet garni, tomato purée, bring to the boil; season to taste, cover and simmer for 1½ hours.
6. Remove bouquet garni. Allow to cool and put into casserole dish.

7. Meantime make the pastry. Roll out an inch larger than dish, cut off one-inch strips of pastry.
8. Arrange the pastry strips around the edge of casserole and brush with cold water.
9. Cover the casserole with the remaining pastry; press down gently around edge to seal.
10. Trim and decorate the edges.
11. With the pastry trimmings roll out and form leaves. After making a hole in the centre of the pastry to allow steam to escape, arrange the leaves around the centre.
12. Brush with beaten egg yolk and set in the oven for 30 minutes until golden brown.
13. Serve garnished with chopped parsley.

To vary:
Substitute ribsteak or shin of beef for roundsteak.

Watchpoint:
When buying lamb's kidney (shaped like a kidney bean) make sure it is plump.

SAVOURY MINCE AND MASH

This is an updated and Irish version of a traditional dish sometimes called shepherd's pie. It is fat and appetizing: full of meat and vegetables with a rich sauce. It is most appreciated when served in winter, piping hot, to people just in from the cold.

Ingredients: Serves: 4–6

1 pint oxtail soup	**500 ml**	2½ cups
1 lb cooked mince	**500 g**	2 cups
2 chopped onions		
1 seeded and chopped green pepper		
1 crushed clove garlic		
1–2 tablespoons tomato purée		
seasoning		
1 lb cooked mashed potato	**450 g**	2 cups
finely chopped parsley		

Preparation time: 20 minutes   **Cooking time:** 20 minutes
Oven position: top   **Oven temperature:** gas 6, 200°C, 400°F

Method:
1. Put the stock, ground meat, onion, pepper, garlic, and tomato purée into a saucepan, bring to a boil, pour out into a deep ovenproof dish.
2. Spread the potatoes on top and run a fork through them for decoration; put into the oven and bake for 20 minutes.
3. Serve hot garnished with chopped parsley.

IRISH SPICED BEEF

This special dish is often found in Irish homes at Christmastime alongside the turkey.

The most important ingredient in a good spiced beef is time. If the spicing is hurried the meat will be tough and indigestible. But if the cooking is started af least a week in advance, the meat will be tender and melting.

Ingredients: Serves: 2-4

6½ lbs beef	3 kg	
3 bay leaves		
9-10 cloves		
5 blades mace		
1 crushed clove garlic		
2 oz brown sugar	50 g	¼ cup
1 lb salt	500 g	2 cups
1 oz saltpetre	25 g	1½ tbsp.
bunch of fresh mixed herbs		
3-4 sliced carrots		
3-4 sliced onions		

Preparation time: 20 minutes; but prepare 7 days in advance of eating.

Cooking time: 5 hours

Method:

1. Wipe meat over with a damp cloth.
2. Mix seasoning ingredients together except for carrots, onions and fresh herbs.
3. Rub seasoning well into meat; then lay meat on bed of seasoning. Leave in a cool place.
4. Repeat rubbing each day.
5. On the seventh day put the meat into a saucepan and cover with cold water.
6. Bring to boiling point and simmer gently for 5 hours, when it should be tender.
7. Put cooked meat on a flat dish and cover with a board. Set weight on top of board until meat is cold, when it is ready to carve and eat.

GUINNESS STEW

The pint of Guinness is a way of life for some Irishmen. The tall blonde lady in the long black skirt is becoming more and more popular in our cooking—especially in stews, pies and flans.

Ingredients: Serves: 4-6

1 lb round steak	500 g
2 tablespoons cooking oil	
3 medium-sized sliced onions	
3-4 sliced carrots	
3-4 stalks of chopped celery	
5-6 sliced potatoes	

2 tablespoons flour
1 pint Guinness or ale   **575 ml**   2½ cups
bouquet garni
salt and freshly ground black pepper
chopped parsley

Preparation time: 25 minutes   **Cooking time:** 2 hours
Oven position: top   **Oven temperature:** gas 6, 200°C, 400°F

Method:

1. Remove any surplus fat from meat and cut into one-inch cubes.
2. Heat the oil in a deep-enough pan (which can later be covered and put in the oven). Fry the meat until golden brown on both sides. Remove from the pan.
3. Put the vegetables in the pan and fry without browning.

    Return meat to pan.
4. Add flour and continue cooking for a further minute.
5. Add the Guinness gradually; bring to the boil, add bouquet garni and season to taste.
6. Cover and place in the oven for two hours.
7. Remove bouquet garni and serve hot, sprinkled with freshly chopped parsley.

MISTY DREAM

This dish, not unlike Beef Stroganoff, uses the tenderest cut—the *fillet mignon*—and is generally cooked and served in a big heavy earthenware dish. A prawn cocktail or a salmon salad would be fine as a starter, and Irish Coffee would be suitable after this substantial meal.

Ingredients: Serves: 4–6

1 lb fillet of beef	**500 g**	
3 medium-sized onions		
8 oz prepared button mushrooms	**225 g**	1½ cups
2 oz butter or margarine	**50 g**	¼ cup
2 tablespoons lemon juice		
¼ pint sour cream	**150 ml**	½ cup
2-3 tablespoons Irish Mist		
salt and black pepper		
finely chopped parsley		
1 lb creamed potatoes	**500**	2 cups

Preparation time: 25 minutes   **Cooking time:** 15 minutes

Method:

1. Cut meat into neat strips 2 inches long by ¼ inch wide. Slice the onion fine.
2. Cut stems of mushrooms off at caps and cut into thin strips downward.

3. Melt half the oil or margarine in a deep frying pan, fry onions and mushrooms for 3 or 4 minutes over a gentle heat, adding more oil or margarine if necessary. Remove these from the pan and keep warm.
4. Add remaining oil or margarine. Allow to get very hot, add beef and fry briskly for 3 or 4 minutes.
5. Put back onions and mushrooms, and cook for 1 or 2 minutes.
6. Over a gentle heat add lemon juice, cream and Irish Mist; mix well together and season to taste.
7. Arrange on serving dish, garnish meat with chopped parsley.
8. Serve with creamed mashed potatoes.

WHISKEY STEAK

This simple but sumptuous dish combines Irish food and drink at their best. Few could afford to eat this well every day; it's a meal for special occasions.

Ingredients: Serves: 1

1 fillet steak
freshly ground black pepper
oil for frying
2 to 3 tablespoons Irish whiskey
2 tablespoons cream
finely chopped parsley

Preparation time: 5 minutes   **Cooking time:** 5–7 minutes
each side

Method:

1. Rub the black pepper into the steak.
2. Heat the oil until it is smoking lightly, add the steak; fry on both sides for 5 or 7 minutes.
3. A minute before cooking is completed, drain off fat and pour on the whiskey. Put a light to the steak and continue cooking for a further minute.
4. Remove steak from heat, and set out on serving plate.
5. Add cream and parsley to the pan, mix well together, pour contents over the steak, and serve hot.

DUBLIN CORNED BEEF AND CABBAGE

This highly flavoured dish was a traditional Sunday lunch for Dubliners. A white savoury sauce was generally made to accompany the corned beef.

There is a choice of two cuts of meat for corned beef: brisket or tail end. The brisket is tougher but is less expensive. The tail end is lean and of very good quality.

The salting process changes the beef from brown to a dark pink colour like that of ham.

Ingredients:

Serves: 6–8

2 lb corned beef brisket or tail end   **1 kg**
a bunch fresh herbs
3–4 sliced carrots
3 sliced onions
6–7 potatoes
1 shredded head of cabbage
horseradish sauce

Preparation time: 20 minutes

Cooking time: 2 hours

Method:

1. If beef is very salty, soak it in cold water for 1 to 2 hours. Drain and cover with cold water.
2. Put into a saucepan, cover with water, bring to the boil, add fresh herbs, and cover the pan. Cook for 1½ hours over a gentle heat.
3. Add vegetables and cook for a further 20 minutes until tender.
4. In the meantime remove the meat and set out on a serving dish and keep warm.
5. Strain liquid off the vegetables.
6. Set vegetables out around the meat and serve with horseradish sauce.

IRISH PORK - The main cuts

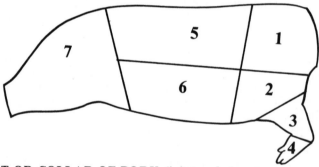

1. **GIGOT OR COLLAR OF PORK** *(joint and chops)*
Medium-priced cuts; joints can be slow-roasted or pot roasted and chops braised.

2. **SHOULDER OF PORK** *(joint)*
A relatively inexpensive cut for roasting, braising and stewing.

3. **FORELEG OR HOCK**
An inexpensive cut ideal for stews or casseroles.

4. **PIG'S FEET OR CRUIBINS**
Very inexpensive and tasty; ideal for stews and casseroles.

80

5. **LOIN OF PORK** *(roast and chops)*
An expensive cut; the joint can be roasted on the bone or boned, rolled and stuffed. Loin chops are good broiled, shallow-fried and braised.

6. **BELLY OF PORK** *(spare ribs)*
A relatively inexpensive cut good for stewing or stuffed and roasted. Separated into smaller units, spare ribs can be roasted, broiled or baked.

7. **LEG OF PORK** *(roast and chops)*
An expensive cut; fresh pork makes a succulent roast and the chops can be broiled, shallow-fried or braised.

SAUSAGE SLICES

This can be a main course for lunch or supper, and when cold is handy for a picnic. Sausage slices go down well with beer—or wine.

Ingredients: Serves: 4–6

8 oz shortcrust pastry	**225 g**	2 cups
12 oz pork sausage meat	**325 g**	1½ cups
1 finely chopped apple		
1 finely chopped onion		
1 teaspoon finely chopped sage		
seasoning		
beaten egg		
chopped parsley		

Preparation time: 20 minutes   **Cooking time:** 25 minutes
Oven position: top   **Oven temperature:** gas 5, 190°C, 375°F

Method:
1. Roll out pastry into a rectangle 12 inches by 10 inches.
2. Combine sausage meat, apple, onion and sage, and season to taste.
3. Spread over the dough, dampen the edges of pastry with cold water and roll up like a jam roll.
4. Cut the roll into slices. Place on a baking sheet and brush with beaten egg. Put in the oven for 25 minutes.
5. Serve hot or cold, garnished with parsley.

CRUIBÍNS

Pronounced "crew-béans," these are trotters or pigs' feet which used to be a staple item for poor Irish who had large families and little money. Cruibíns are eaten today partly out of nostalgia, but mostly for the eating that's in them: the sheer pleasure of a meat that can be picked up in the hands and the bones licked clean. Cruibíns are still very cheap. When last priced in a butcher shop they were six pence a piece.

They are served in some country pubs on Fridays and Saturdays, and are more delicious when washed down with ample draughts of beer or porter.

Ingredients: Serves: 4–6

6 pigs feet
a bunch fresh herbs
8 oz fresh vegetables
   (carrots, onions, white turnips)   **250 g**   2 cups
mustard sauce
griddle bread or soda bread
   and butter (to serve)

Preparation time: 15 minutes   **Cooking time:** 2½–3 hours

Method:

1. Wash the cruibíns and put into a saucepan of cold water with vegetables, cover and bring to the boil.
2. Simmer for at least 2½ hours, so that the meat comes away from the bone.
3. Drain off liquid and reserve for soup (vegetables used here for flavour only). Serve cruibíns hot with mustard sauce and fresh buttered bread.

DUBLIN CODDLE

This was a real Dubliners' dish (though it's not as popular today as it was thirty or forty years ago) and made a very satisfying winter meal. Rashers, sausages, onions and potatoes were put into a saucepan and covered with water, although some people substituted milk for water to enrich it or thickened it with flour or cornflour. Adding a few spare ribs to the pot did no harm at all. Coddle was a great favourite, especially with the ordinary people of the city. Coddling meant soaking water just below the boiling point.

Ingredients: Serves: 6

1 lb rashers   **500 g**
1 lb sausages   **500 g**
6 sliced onions
8–10 thinly sliced potatoes
2 cooking apples
   (peeled, cored and sliced)
a bunch fresh herbs
pepper
1 pint vegetable stock or water   **500 ml**   2½ cups
finely chopped parsley
fresh crusty bread or rolls (to serve)

Preparation time: 20 minutes   **Cooking time:** 45 minutes

Method:

1. Remove rind from the rashers and cut into 3 pieces.

82

2. Layer meat, vegetables and apples in a saucepan. Add fresh herbs and pepper to taste.
3. Pour stock or water over, and cover.
4. Bring to the boil over a gentle heat and simmer for 40 to 45 minutes until vegetables are tender.
5. Serve hot, sprinkled with parsley, and eat with fresh bread or rolls.

PORK AND APPLE STEW

Large and meaty chops are ideal for this basic Irish farmers' meal.

Ingredients: Serves: 6

1 oz butter or margarine	25 g	1½ tbsp.
6 trimmed pork chops		
8 small onions		
3 green apples		
(peeled, cored and sliced)		
2 oz sultanas	50 g	⅓ cup
½ pint stock or water	275 ml	1¼ cups
pinch of nutmeg		
bouquet garni		
salt and black pepper		
½ oz brown sugar	15 g	1 tbsp.
1 tablespoon currant jelly		
finely chopped parsley		

Preparation time 25 minutes   **Cooking time:** 1 hour
Oven position: top   **Oven temperature:** gas 6, 200°C, 400°F

Method:
1. Heat margarine or butter in an ovenproof pan or dish on stove. Brown the chops on both sides.
2. Arrange onions, apples and sultanas on top of chops.
3. Pour on the stock, add nutmeg, bouquet garni and season to taste.
4. Sprinkle with brown sugar.
5. Cover and place in the oven for an hour.
6. When cooked, remove bouquet garni and stir currant jelly into the stew.
7. Garnish with parsley and serve hot.

LEINSTER CHOPS

Some of the best pork in Ireland comes from the lush feeding grounds of the province of Leinster in the east and southeast of Ireland.

Ingredients: Serves: 4

2 oz butter or margarine	50 g	¼ cup
4 loin pork chops		
10 oz apricots	275 g	1¼ cups

½ teaspoon ginger		
2 oz sugar	**50 g**	¼ cup
juice and rind of a lemon		
salt and black pepper		
finely chopped parsley		

Preparation time: 20 minutes   **Cooking time:** 20 minutes

Method:

1. Heat the fat and fry the chops allowing 7 to 10 minutes for each side.
2. Put the apricots, ginger, sugar, rind and juice of lemon into a saucepan and simmer for 15 minutes.
3. Liquidize or put through a sieve.
4. Arrange the pork chops on a serving dish, spoon a little sauce over them.
5. Garnish with chopped parsley.
6. Serve remaining sauce in a sauceboat.

Watchpoint:

The colour of the lean pork will vary according to the age of the pig. The lean meat, pink in an older pig, is almost white in the tender young suckling.

PIG'S RINGS

There is no fat in the fillet, the leanest cut of pork, which is the basis for this delicious stuffed main dish.

Ingredients: Serves: 4

2 large pork steaks		
filling:		
4 oz breadcrumbs	**100 g**	2 cups
1 oz grated walnuts	**25 g**	¼ cup
1 teaspoon chopped fresh thyme		
8 oz mandarin oranges	**225 g**	1 cup
2 tablespoons oil		
walnut sauce:		
8 oz mandarin oranges	**225 g**	1 cup
8 oz grated walnuts	**225 g**	1¾ cups
rind of nutmeg		
finely chopped parsley		

Preparation time: 15 minutes   **Cooking time:** 45 minutes
Oven position: top   **Oven temperature:** gas 6, 200°C, 400°F

Method for stuffed fillet:

1. Cut pork steaks in half, and lay them out on a working board or table.
2. Prepare the stuffing: put breadcrumbs, walnuts, thyme and drained oranges into a bowl; add enough juice from oranges to bind the stuffing.
3. Divide the stuffing evenly between the pork fillets; lay stuf-

84

fing on top of each steak, roll up and secure with skewer.

4. Put into a roasting tin with oil; pour remaining juices over steaks, cover them and put into the oven for 45 minutes to 1 hour. Baste during cooking.

Method for walnut sauce:
1. Liquidize mandarin oranges.

2. Put grated walnuts, nutmeg and mandarin oranges into a saucepan and bring to the boil.
3. Pour sauce into a sauceboat.
4. Arrange meat on serving dish; spoon a little sauce over it, garnish with finely chopped parsley and serve hot.

SPICY SPARE RIBS

In Ireland in the past spare ribs were generally boiled or roasted. People ate them with their hands, the gentry using finger bowls and linen napkins; the poor licking their fingers. Ribs are often served at banquets in our old castles. This is a kind of sweet and sour dish.

Ingredients: Serves: 4–6

2 lbs spare ribs	1 kg	
½ pint stock or water	275 ml	1¼ cups
4 oz brown sugar	100 g	½ cup
½ pint vinegar	275 ml	1¼ cups
3 tablespoons soya sauce		
2 finely chopped onions		
salt and black pepper		
½ oz cornflour (cornstarch) blended		
with 1–2 tablespoons milk	10 g	1 tbsp.

Preparation time: 20 minutes   **Cooking time:** 1¼–1½ hours
Oven position: centre   **Oven temperature:** gas 6, 200°C, 400°F

Method:
1. Arrange spare ribs in an ovenproof dish.
2. Mix all ingredients together, except cornflour.
3. Pour over spare ribs, cover and

set in the oven for 1¼ hours.
4. Thicken sauce with cornstarch, spoon over spare ribs.
5. Set spare ribs out on a platter and serve hot.

IRISH BACON - The main cuts

1. COLLAR OF BACON *(joints)*
A medium-priced cut good for boiling, braising or stewing.

2. SHOULDER OF BACON *(joints)*
An inexpensive cut providing bacon joints for boiling.

3. STREAKY RASHERS *(slices)*
A relatively inexpensive cut from which the more fatty—streaky—

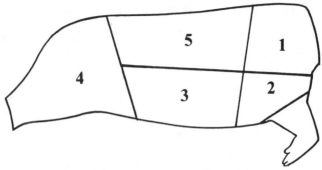

slices are obtained. These can be fried or grilled.

4. GAMMON *(joints, steak cuts)*
The most expensive cuts come from the gammon or leg. These cuts can be roasted (roast ham) or boiled; gammon or ham steaks can also be cut for frying.

5. BACK RASHERS *(slices)*
A more expensive cut—the lean slices are taken from the back and are ideal for grilling and frying.

ENNISCORTHY BOILED BACON

Enniscorthy is a town in County Wexford—"the model county"—and one of the sunniest in Ireland. Enniscorthy is famous for its barley-fed bacon, which is boiled as a joint and usually served with cabbage to make a meal especially popular during harvest time.

As a matter interest there are several different kinds of joints of cured ham on the Irish market. Sweet cured bacon or ham is very mild and does not need soaking before cooking. Unsmoked or green bacon, also very mild in flavour, needs little or no soaking before use. Smoked bacon is saltier, and must be put into cold water and soaked overnight; often the water is strained off, the joint is put into a saucepan and covered with cold water or to vary the flavour half water and half cider or ginger ale.

Ingredients:	Serves: 6
2 lbs bacon	**1 kg**
cold water	
1 teaspoon mustard	
boiled cabbage	
½ pint parsley sauce	**275 ml**
1¼ cups	

Preparation time: 10 minutes　　　　**Cooking time:** 1 hour

Method:

1. Wash the bacon. If very salty put steeping for a few hours in cold water. Rinse in cold water.
2. Put into a pot and cover with cold water, bring slowly to the boil, skim and boil for 5 minutes, then simmer gently for 50 to 60 minutes.
3. When cooked, remove the rind from the bacon and coat the fat with mustard.
4. Carve bacon and arrange on serving dish. Arrange cabbage around the edge of dish and pour parsley sauce into a sauceboat. Serve hot.

GAMMON STEAKS LOCH GORMAN

Pig meat should always be cooked slowly, whatever method is used. This is not just for safety. Pork and ham need time to bring out their natural richness. Strong flavourings like ginger, garlic, rosemary and sage complement any pork or ham dish. A good acidy sauce, made for example from apples or gooseberries, lightens the meat.

Gammon steak—or ham steak—is relatively new to the Irish market but very popular because it is so good and easy to prepare. It has little fat and a fine texture and is generally grilled.

Ingredients: Serves: 2

2 gammon steaks
1 dessert apple
1½ oz butter or margarine   **40 g**   2 tbsp.
¼ pint yoghurt   **150 ml**   ½ cup
paprika
peas
chips

Preparation time: 5 minutes   **Cooking time:** 15 minutes

Method:

1. Heat the grill and place steaks on grill pan. Grill each side for 5 to 7 minutes.
2. In the meantime, peel, core, and cut the apple horizontally into rings (4 even-sized rings).
3. Melt the margarine in a frying pan and fry the apples carefully (avoid breaking) in the fat for 2 to 3 minutes on either side.
4. Place steaks on serving dish. Arrange 2 apple rings on each steak. Pour yoghurt over apples.
5. Shake a little paprika over.
6. Serve immediately, garnished with peas.

BAKED LIMERICK HAM

What makes ham expensive is its leanness and superior quality. Hams are taken from the leg and can be bought pale or smoked. Limerick Ham is famous because of the quality of the pigs reared in the rich dairy farming region of the Golden Vale in east County Limerick and in Tipperary: pigs thrive on skim milk.

Ingredients: Serves: 8–10

2 lb ham   1 kg
4 sticks celery
bouquet garni
1 teaspoon mustard
16 oz apricots   500 g   2 cups
2–3 tablespoons lightly whipped
   cream

Preparation time: 10 minutes   **Cooking time:** 1½ hours
Oven position: top   **Oven temperature:** gas 6, 200°C, 400°F

Method:

1. Put the ham, celery and bouquet garni into a saucepan and cover with cold water; bring to the boil over a gentle heat; skim, cover and simmer for 1 hour.
2. Remove ham from water, peel off rind and score ham fat in diamonds. Coat fat with mustard and put in a baking tin.
3. Pour half the juice from the apricots over the ham and cover with tinfoil; put into oven and bake for a further 30 minutes.
4. Reserve 3 or 4 apricots; press remaining apricots through a sieve and pour sieved apricots into a bowl; pour on remaining apricot juice and cream and mix well together. Put this sauce into a sauceboat.
5. Carve ham, arranging slices on serving dish, garnish with apricots reserved earlier.
6. Serve with apricot sauce.

ROLLED STUFFED VEAL

Veal is the meat from beef calf. The meat is very tender but lacks flavour, so it needs a good stuffing or sauce to enhance it. Because it lacks fat, it needs to be basted often during the cooking.

Ingredients: Serves: 8–10

4 lbs loin of veal   2 kg
8 oz sausage meat   225 g   1 cup
8 oz spinach   225 g   2 cups
4 medium-sized onions
1 crushed clove garlic
4 oz breadcrumbs   100 g   2 cups
seasoning
2–3 tablespoons stock
2 tablespoons oil

Preparation time: 20 minutes   **Cooking time:** 1½ hours
Oven position: centre   **Oven temperature:**
                              gas 5, 190°C, 375°F

Method:
1. Place the meat on board or worktop.
2. Put the spinach into salted boiling water; cook for ten minutes, strain and chop.
3. Put sausage meat, spinach, onions, crushed garlic and bread-crumbs into a bowl and mix well together. Season to taste and bind with stock.
4. Arrange the stuffing in the centre of the slab of veal.
5. Roll up tightly and tie. Heat the oil in baking tin.
6. Put the meat into the baking tin and baste during cooking for about 1½ hours.
7. Carve and serve on oval shaped dish.

Watchpoint:
Veal should be pale rosy pink in colour.

WEIGHTS AND MEASURES

An important point to remember with regard to solid measures. Irish cooks are generous with their teaspoon and tablespoon measures: these are usually heaped, while the American cook levels off the quantity on the spoon with a knife. So it is important to note that where a recipe specifies a teaspoon of sugar, for example, you should use a rounded teaspoonful, i.e. as much above the spoon as in it, or **two** level teaspoonfuls.

Poultry and Game

Driving into Tomadilly yard we have to slow down for fear a hen will cut across the path of the car. During the summer months the front gates leading to the driveway and garden are always closed to keep the fowl from eating mother's flowers.

When we were children we had a chicken house, a hen house, a duck house and a turkey house. The geese were put into any spare house available. The ducks with their lovely big breasts preferred to waddle around the water tank. The few geese we kept loved the long grass in the field nearby, and had to be watched closely for fear a fox would steal one. It was in August or September that the young goslings were born; the little yellow creatures would seem to swim along behind their mother through the stubbled field. The turkeys, bought from a hatchery or from a farmer's wife during July or August, were kept in the house until they were eleven or twelve weeks old, then allowed out into the yard where they'd noisily stretch themselves as if they'd never slept in their lives. When the shooting season started—on the first of November in Ireland—we'd manage to pot a few pheasants. The problem was that they always looked too nice to pluck.

COTTAGE CHICKEN

This is a beautiful dish, full of flavour, which works well even with the battery chickens often used today. In times past a dish like this would be cooked in a big black three-legged pot hanging from a bar over a blazing turf fire.

Ingredients: Serves: 6

3½ lb chicken   1.5 kg
6 medium-sized onions
6 medium-sized carrots
6 small potatoes
1 crushed clove garlic
juice and rind of 1 orange
½ pint chicken stock   250 ml   1½ cups
bouquet garni
seasoning
1 tablespoon cornflour
2 tablespoons milk
finely chopped parsley

Preparation time: 20 minutes   **Cooking time:** 1½ hours
Oven position: top   **Oven temperature:** gas 6, 200°C, 400°F

Method:

1. Wash and dry the chicken well and put into a large casserole.
2. Prepare vegetables according to kind, slice onions and carrots into half-inch rings, cut potatoes in two.
3. Put the vegetables, garlic and orange rind into the casserole, lining them around the chicken.
4. Pour the orange juice and stock over; season to taste and add bouquet garni.
5. Cover casserole and put it into the oven for 1½ hours.
6. Remove casserole from oven and carve chicken.
7. Set out on serving dish, arranging vegetables neatly around the chicken. Remove bouquet garni from casserole.
8. Blend corn with milk and add to juices, bring to the boil, stirring continuously and season to taste.
9. Spoon a little stock over the chicken; pour remainder into sauceboat.
10. Serve hot, garnished with parsley.

CHICKEN LOAF

This is an ideal way of using leftover chicken—or any other fowl for that matter. It can be served hot or cold and is perfect for a buffet party or a picnic basket.

Ingredients: Serves: 4–6

1 lb cooked diced chicken	**500 g**	2 cups
½ lb sausage meat	**225 g**	1 cup
1 seeded and finely chopped green pepper		
2 medium-sized finely chopped onions		
2 teaspoons finely chopped fresh herbs		
1 crushed clove garlic		
4 oz breadcrumbs	**100 g**	2 cups
1 oz chopped nuts	**25 g**	¼ cup
½ pint chicken stock	**275 ml**	1¼ cups
seasoning		

Preparation time: 20 minutes
Oven position: centre

Cooking time: 1 hour
Oven temperature:
gas 5, 190°C, 375°F

Method:

1. Prepare meat and vegetables.
2. Put all ingredients into a bowl, mix well, bind with stock, and season to taste.

91

3. Mould into loaf shape, set on a greased baking sheet and bake in oven.

4. Serve hot or cold.

CHICKEN PLANT

Chicken has very little fat and so needs to be basted regularly, and is very good while cooked in a highly flavoured sauce such as that suggested here.

Aubergines or egg plants, when coated and fired, produce a very rich crisp base which when filled with this substantial sauce creates a fine main course for a dinner menu.

Ingredients: Serves: 6

2 lbs aubergines	**1 kg**		
salt and pepper			
1 oz flour	**25 g**	¼ cup	
2 oz butter or margarine	**50 g**	¼ cup	
filling:			
1 oz butter or margarine	**25 g**	1½ tbsp.	
2 finely chopped onions			
6 oz sliced mushrooms	**175 g**	1¼ cups	
12 oz cooked sliced chicken	**325 g**	1½ cups	
1 tablespoon tomato purée			
1 crushed clove garlic			
1–2 teaspoons finely chopped parsley			
¼ pint chicken stock	**150 ml**	½ cup	
topping:			
4 oz breadcrumbs	**100 g**	2 cups	
2 oz melted butter or margarine	**50 g**	¼ cup	

Preparation time: 20 minutes   **Cooking time:** 20–25 minutes
Oven position: top   **Oven temperature:** gas 6, 200°C, 400°F

Method for aubergines:

1. Cut the aubergines in half on the length, salt and flour them, melt the fat and fry them for 7 or 8 minutes until golden brown, place on a wire tray.

Method for filling:

1. Melt the butter or margarine in a saucepan; gently fry the onions and mushrooms.
2. Add the cooked chicken, tomato purée, garlic, chopped parsley, a little stock and season to taste.
3. Remove the centre seeds from each aubergine with a spoon and place in a casserole. Fill with the chicken mixture.
4. Sprinkle with breadcrumbs, and pour fat over the breadcrumbs.
5. Pour a little stock around the aubergines.
6. Place in the oven and bake for 20 to 25 minutes.
7. Serve hot.

92

CHICKEN PUFF

The chicken puff is a non-traditional dish, but it's splendid for parties. It always looks very good and is not all that difficult to prepare.

Ingredients: Serves: 4–6

8 oz puff pastry	225 g	2 cups
beaten egg		
filling:		
1 oz butter or margarine	25 g	1½ tbsp.
2 sliced onions		
1 oz flour	25 g	¼ cup
½ pint milk	275 ml	1¼ cups
1 lb diced cooked chicken	½ kg	2 cups
8 oz mushrooms	225 g	1½ cups
4 seeded and skinned tomatoes		
finely chopped parsley		

Preparation time: 30 minutes   **Cooking time:** 25 minutes
Oven position: top   **Oven temperature:** gas 7, 220°C, 425°F

Method for pastry shell:

1. Roll out puff pastry to a half-inch thickness.
2. Put a plate eight inches in diameter on top of pastry and cut around it with a knife, holding the knife slantwise to form a bevelled edge wider at the base. Turn this cutout upside down onto a dampened baking sheet so that the widest part is on top.
3. With a cutter (or a plate) mark a circle seven inches in diameter with the back of the knife. Brush with beaten egg (avoid brushing sides). Place in the oven.
4. In 25 minutes the pastry should be well risen and a good colour. Then it can be slid out onto a wire tray to cool. While the pastry shell is still warm, lift off the top by cutting around the circle mark with the point of a small knife. Set onto a serving dish before filling.

Method for filling:

1. Melt the butter or margarine, fry onions until soft, add the flour and blend well together, add the milk and bring to the boil stirring continuously.
2. Add diced chicken, mushrooms and tomatoes, bring back to the boil and season to taste. Simmer for 20 minutes.
3. Place filling in the centre of pastry shell and set top of pastry removed earlier over filling.
4. Garnish with finely chopped parsley, and serve hot if possible.

To vary:

Fix in the form of several small puffs, using a pastry mould or a cup to shape the shell.

DRESSY LADY

This is a lively casserole, in which a traditional Irish stew recipe is varied by using wine.

Ingredients: Serves: 6

2 tablespoons oil		
1 large chicken divided into 6 portions		
12 button onions (skinned and chopped)		
4 oz chopped gammon rashers	100 g	⅔ cup
8 oz button mushrooms	225 g	1½ cups
4 tomatoes (skinned and halved)		
2 tablespoons tomato purée		
½ pint chicken stock	275 ml	1¼ cups
1 crushed clove garlic		
½ pint red wine	275 ml	1¼ cups
seasoning		
1 tablespoon cornflour		
1 tablespoon finely chopped parsley		

Preparation time: 20 minutes   **Cooking time:** 1½ hours
Oven position: centre   **Oven temperature:**
                                    gas 5, 190°C, 375°F

Method:

1. Heat the oil; fry the chicken joints until golden brown on both sides. Remove from pan and place in a casserole.
2. Fry onions, gammon rashers, mushrooms and tomatoes for 2 minutes over a gentle heat. Remove to the casserole.
3. Blend the tomato purée with stock and garlic, add wine, season to taste, and pour over chicken and vegetables.
4. Cover and put in oven, cook for 1¼ hours.
5. Blend the cornflour with a little stock, pour into casserole and continue cooking for a further 15 minutes.
6. Serve hot sprinkled with chopped parsley.

GALLOPING HORSESHOE

An Irish horseshoe is a symbol of good luck; the old stables always had a horseshoe nailed to the door. This dish has that same lucky look, and is very satisfying besides.

Ingredients: Serves: 4–6

8 oz shortcrust pastry	225 g	2 cups

filling:

1 oz margarine	**25 g**	1½ tbsp.
2 finely chopped onions		
3–4 skinned and sliced tomatoes		
1 teaspoon sage		
1 oz flour	**25 g**	¼ cup
¼ pint milk	**150 ml**	½ cup
4 oz cooked turkey or chicken	**100 g**	½ cup
2 oz cooked vegetables	**50 g**	½ cup
seasoning		
a little milk		
finely chopped parsley		

Preparation time: 20 minutes   **Cooking time:** 30–35 minutes
Oven position: top   **Oven temperature:** gas 6, 200°C, 400°F

Method:

1. Make shortcrust pastry, and let rest in refrigerator.
2. Melt the margarine in a saucepan, fry the onions lightly, add tomatoes and sage, beat in the flour and cook for a minute. Add the milk, then the turkey and vegetables, and bring to the boil. Season to taste. Allow to cool.
3. Turn pastry onto a floured board and knead lightly.
4. Roll into a rectangular shape 10 by 14 inches.
5. Arrange filling on the pastry (avoid putting filling too close to the edge).
6. Dampen edges with water and roll up. Shape into horseshoe, place on a baking sheet.
7. Brush pastry with a little milk, and bake.
8. Serve hot or cold garnished with chopped parsley.

ROAST CHICKEN

Chicken was a very special dish in Ireland until a few years ago and was served only on special occasions. Today chicken is plentiful and popular.

When we were children, chickens were reared in almost every country house. Bought when one or two day old chicks, they were fed chiefly on meal and milk; as they got bigger they were let run free in the farmyard and pick up grains of corn and scraps of bread. Killed when ten to twelve weeks old, these chickens had fine big breasts and were delicious roasted.

Ingredients: Serves: 4–6

chicken:

1 oz butter or margarine	**25 g**	1½ tbsp.
1 roasting chicken		
¾ pint stock	**450 ml**	2 cups
1 chopped onion		

95

½ oz flour	**15 g**	1 tbsp.
1 seeded and chopped pepper		
rice:		
1 oz butter	**25 g**	1½ tbsp.
1 sliced onion		
2 oz raisins	**50 g**	⅔ cup
5 oz rice	**150 g**	1 cup
1 chopped clove garlic		
¾ pint stock	**450 ml**	2 cups
knobs of butter		
finely chopped parsley		

Preparation time: 20 minutes   **Cooking time:**
1 hour 20 minutes
Oven position: top   **Oven temperature:** gas 6, 200°C, 400°F

Method for cooking chicken:

1. Melt butter or margarine in a saucepan. Put chicken into a casserole, pour melted butter or margarine and stock over the chicken.
2. Set into the oven and bake for 1 hour and 20 minutes; baste chicken every 15 minutes, and turn from time to time.

Method for cooking rice:

1. Melt margarine in a heavy casserole, add onion, soften over a gentle heat but do not brown.
2. Add raisins, rice, garlic and stock, cook for 4 to 5 minutes, bring to the boil, season, cover the pan and cook in the oven for 20 to 25 minutes, when the rice should be tender and the stock absorbed.

3. With a fork stir in a knob of butter.

Method for serving roasted chicken:

1. Remove chicken from casserole, carve and set on a serving dish (keep hot).
2. Skim gravy, put 2 tablespoons of gravy into a saucepan, put over a moderate heat, add onion and soften. Stir in the flour and cook for a minute. Add stock; bring to the boil, stirring continuously.
3. Add chopped pepper and cook for 5 to 6 minutes.
4. Spoon gravy over the chicken. Sprinkle with chopped parsley and serve with savoury rice.

To vary:

Use stuffing, as in Christmas dinner recipe below.

CHRISTMAS TURKEY

Roast stuffed turkey has become as typical a Christmas dinner in Ireland as in America. Many farm wives rear a dozen free-range turkeys for gifts to friends at Christmastime, hanging them about a week before the big day.

Ingredients:
Serves: 24

14 lb turkey	6.5 kg	
stuffing:		
10 oz white breadcrumbs	275 g	5 cups
½ lb sausage meat	225 g	1 cup
4 oz streaky rashers	100 g	⅔ cup
1–2 teaspoons chopped parsley		
16 oz tin apricots	500 g	2 cups
seasoning		
4–5 slices streaky rashers		
½ pint turkey stock	275 ml	1¼ cups
1 finely chopped onion		
1 tablespoon flour		

Preparation time: 25 minutes **Cooking time:** 4 hours
Oven position: centre **Oven temperature:** gas 4 to 5, 180°
to 190°C, 350° to 375°F

Method:

1. Wash the turkey well and dry.
2. Put breadcrumbs, sausage meat, chopped bacon, parsley and half the chopped apricots into a bowl; season to taste.
3. Bind with apricot juice from tin.
4. Stuff the bird with this. Place on its side in the baking tin and cover the breast with streaky rashers.
5. Pour turkey stock into pan, cover with tinfoil and place in oven.
6. Baste the turkey every 20 minutes with stock. After two hours turn turkey over onto its other side.
7. Place the chopped onion in the pan 15 minutes before cooking is completed.
8. Remove turkey from the pan, blend flour with a little stock, add to pan and bring to the boil, stirring continuously; season to taste, cook for 5 minutes and strain into sauce boat.
9. Decorate turkey with remaining apricots.
10. Serve each guest a piece of brown meat along with the white.

To vary:

Use celery and walnuts—or chestnuts, almonds or cashews. Or use apples and apple juice. A dash of orange or pineapple juice can be added if no other fruit is used. Or use potato stuffing as in the goose dinner below.

Watchpoint:

Hen turkeys are smaller in size than cocks, which can weigh up to thirty pounds. Hens never weigh more than sixteen pounds and their meat is much juicier and far more tender.

97

TURKEY PIE

Because people tend to buy large turkeys at Christmastime, there is always plenty of cooked cold turkey afterward; and a pie is one of the best ways of using up the leftovers. This pie, cooked in a highly flavoured sauce, is covered with a rich crust of pastry.

Ingredients: Serves: 4–6

8 oz rough puff or flaky pastry	**225 g**	2 cups
1 pint chicken soup	**500 ml**	2½ cups
4 oz peas	**100 g**	⅔ cup
1 lb cooked sliced turkey	**500 g**	2 cups
2 finely chopped onions		
seasoning		
beaten egg or milk		
sprigs of parsley		

Preparation time: 25 minutes   **Cooking time:** 25 minutes
Cooking time: top   **Oven temperature:** gas 6–7, 200°–220°C, 400°–425°F

Method:

1. Roll out pastry to half an inch thickness to cover a medium casserole.
3. Cover casserole with pastry.
4. Flake and decorate the edge of pastry.
5. Glaze with beaten egg or milk. Set into the oven and cook for 25 minutes.
6. Serve hot, garnished with parsley.

GOLDEN GOOSE

While Irish turkey provided the centrepiece for the festive meal in most Irish households, our specialty at home was goose. Each year we fed three young goslings on bread, meal, milk, and fattened them on the long grass "down the park" i.e. in the nearby field. We kept a close watch for fear a fox would eat them. We ate our first holiday goose at Christmas, the second on New Year's Day and the third on Little Christmas, the 6th of January.

Ingredients: Serves: 8–10

10 lb oven-ready goose	**4.5 kg**	
stuffing:		
2 oz butter	**50 g**	¼ cup
¼ pint milk	**150 ml**	⅝ cup
1 lb cooked mashed potatoes	**500 g**	2 cups
2 finely chopped onions		
1–2 teaspoons mixed herbs		

salt and freshly ground black pepper
gravy:
finely chopped onion
1 teaspoon finely chopped herbs
$\frac{1}{2}$ pint stock   **250 ml** $1\frac{1}{2}$ cups

Preparation time: 30 minutes   **Cooking time:** $2\frac{1}{2}$–3 hours
Oven position: centre   **Oven temperature:**
gas 6, 200°C, 400°F

Method:
1. Cut off the neck close to the body; remove entrails and excess fat from the cavity. Remove feet and ends of wings at the first joint.
2. To make the stuffing, heat butter and milk in a saucepan. Add the mashed potatoes, onion and herbs. Mix well together and season to taste.
3. Stuff the goose with savoury potato stuffing.
4. Put the goose into a roasting tin and cover with tinfoil. Put in the oven.
5. Put finely chopped onion into the roasting tin 15 minutes before cooking is completed.
6. Remove goose from the tin when roasted, and keep hot.
7. Strain off fat, reserving 1 tablespoon of it along with onion in roasting tin. Add seasoning, herbs and stock.
8. Bring to boil, strain and serve in sauce jug.
9. Carve goose and arrange, garnished with parsley, on preheated serving dish.

Watchpoint:
It is a good idea to prepare separately the goose and the stuffing the night before cooking, covering them after preparation.

CREAMY PHEASANT

In November the shooting season starts when most pheasants are killed for the table. Some people hang pheasant by the neck after killing. But Irish hunters tell us that the thing to do is to hang a pheasant for ten days by one leg from a line or a ceiling rack. This allows the blood to flow evenly throughout the body and the air to circulate around it. Shaking pepper on feathers keeps flies away.

The meat of a pheasant is dark and rich and is best served with a stuffing or in a creamy sauce.

Ingredients: **Serves: 6**

1 pheasant'
2 tablespoons oil
1 medium-sized chopped onion
2 slices chopped streaky rashers
1 oz flour   **25 g** $\frac{1}{4}$ cup

1 pint stock	**500 ml**	2½ cups
2 chopped apples		
4 oz sliced carrots	**100 g**	1 cup
½ pint yoghurt	**250 ml**	1½ cups
¼ pint cream	**150 ml**	½ cup
finely chopped parsley		
6–8 fried apple rings		

Preparation time: 25 minutes   **Cooking time:** 1 hour
Oven position: top   **Oven temperature:** gas 6, 200°C, 400°F

Method:

1. Joint the pheasant.
2. Heat oil in a heavy casserole, fry the joints for a minute on either side, remove from the pan and fry the onion and bacon lightly.
3. Add flour, cook for a minute, gradually add the stock, bring to the boil stirring continuously.
4. Add apples, carrots and meat joints.
5. Bring back to the boil, cover and place in the oven.
6. When cooked, remove joints and place on serving dish, arrange the rashers and vegetables around the joints. Keep hot.
7. Strain the juice and put back into the casserole, bring to the boil, add the yoghurt or cream. Pour over meat and vegetables.
8. Serve hot garnished with fried apple rings.
9. Sprinkle with chopped parsley.

RABBIT STEW

Rabbits are plentiful in Ireland. At home when the barley and wheat are being gathered we would often see them hopping along in front of the combine harvester. Rabbits were a menace in the vegetable garden, particularly to cabbage plants.

Rabbits can be roasted. But they make a fine appetizing stew.

Ingredients: Serves: 4–6

1 rabbit		
1½ oz butter or margarine	**50 g**	2 tbsp.
3 sliced onions		
1 oz flour	**25 g**	¼ cup
¾ pint stock	**425 ml**	2 cups
juice of lemon		
3 sliced carrots		
4 oz mushrooms	**100 g**	¾ cup
seasoning		
lemon strips		

Preparation time: 30 minutes   **Cooking time:** 1½ hours
Oven position: top   **Oven temperature:** gas 6, 200°C, 400°F

Method:

1. Wash, dry and joint the rabbit.
2. Melt fat in earthenware casserole and fry rabbit on either side for 1 minute, then remove from the casserole.
3. Fry the onions gently, add flour and cook for a minute; add the stock and lemon juice and bring to the boil, stirring continuously.
4. Add carrots and rabbit, bring back to boiling point, season to taste.
5. Put lid on casserole and set it into the oven for 1½ hours.
6. 15 minutes before cooking is completed, add the mushrooms.
7. Arrange meat and vegetables on serving dish, garnish with strips of lemon and serve hot.

WEIGHTS AND MEASURES

An important point to remember with regard to solid measures. Irish cooks are generous with their teaspoon and tablespoon measures: these are usually heaped, while the American cook levels off the quantity on the spoon with a knife. So it is important to note that where a recipe specifies a teaspoon of sugar, for example, you should use a rounded teaspoonful, i.e. as much above the spoon as in it, or **two** level teaspoonfuls.

101

Vegetables

COLCANNON

This was the centrepiece of the traditional harvest dinner: a lunch some Americans would call it, but there was more than lunching in this delicious dish. It was served at midday, which on the slower Irish clock meant one in the afternoon.

There was a body and flavour and aroma about colcannon that was something all its own. The very thought of it must have hauled the men down from the tractors and combines and pulled them away from the sheaves like a taut invisible wire. Colcannon began with a mixture of raw white vegetables, heavily seasoned and layered in giant saucepans. Then water was poured over it, and the heavy lids shut tight with handirons or anything else weighty enough to prevent them from popping. It took about half an hour to cook. Hugh servings were dished out to the men, who made hollows in the centre of the steaming hot colcannon and filled the hollows with lashings of country butter; they used huge spoons in eating it.

Colcannon was a Hallowe'en dish, too. Coins were wrapped in foil and buried in the colcannon, and children would eat their way in to where the coins were hidden.

Ingredients: Serves: 4–6

1 medium-sized head white cabbage
2 medium-sized parsnips
3–4 medium-sized onions
8–10 medium-sized potatoes
salt and pepper
1 pint water   **500 ml**   2½ cups
4 oz butter   **100 g**   ½ cup

Preparation time: 20 minutes   **Cooking time:** 25–30 minutes

Method:

1. Cut cabbage into four, remove stumps and wash each leaf thoroughly in salt and water. Put four or five outer leaves aside, chop the remaining leaves finely.

2. Wash and scrape parsnips, remove skins from the onions.

3. Cut parsnips, onions and potatoes into half-inch slices.

4. Arrange a layer of potatoes in the bottom of a saucepan, cover with a layer of parsnips, then a layer of onions, then a layer of cabbage; season well, continue layering the vegetables, and again season well.

5. Pour water over the vegetables and cover vegetables completely with the outer leaves. Put the lid

102

on the saucepan, bring to the boil and cover; simmer until cooked.

6. Strain off any excess water. Remove the outer leaves of cabbage. Mash the vegetables well, add the butter and mix well. Put into a serving dish.
7. Serve hot with plenty of creamy butter.

Watchpoints:
For vegetables generally, there is an easy guide to cooking: (1) All vegetables grown above ground are cooked quickly in salted boiling water. Examples: cabbage, cauliflower, spinach, peas, corn, asparagus; (2) Vegetables grown under the ground are covered in salted cold water and then cooked slowly. Examples: potatoes, turnips, carrots, onions.

The only cabbage to use in colcannon is white cabbage.

CHAMP

This is a fine substantial Irish vegetable dish made from mashed potatoes and scallions.

Ingredients:		Serves: 4
2 oz melted butter	50 g	$\frac{1}{4}$ cup
$\frac{1}{4}$ pint milk	150 ml	$\frac{5}{8}$ cup
2 oz finely chopped scallions	50 g	$\frac{1}{4}$ cup
1 lb mashed potatoes	500 g	2 cups
salt and pepper		
4 oz butter	100 g	$\frac{1}{2}$ cup

Preparation time: 20 minutes   **Cooking time:** 5 minutes

Method:

1. Put butter, milk and scallions into a saucepan, bring to the boil and simmer for 2 or 3 minutes.
2. Add the potatoes and mix well together.
3. Simmer for 5 minutes over a gentle heat and season to taste.
4. Put into a serving dish, make a hole in the centre and drop in the butter.

BOXTY

This is a traditional recipe in counties like Donegal, Leitrim and Cavan. Equal quantities of raw potatoes, cooked potatoes and flour are mixed together. Then spoonfuls of the mixture are put onto a well-greased pan and baked until golden on both sides.

Ingredients:		Serves: 4–6
8 oz grated raw potatoes	225 g	1 cup
8 oz mashed potatoes	225 g	1 cup

4 oz plain flour	**100 g**	1 cup
2 oz butter	**50 g**	¼ cup
pinch of salt		
butter or margarine for frying		

Preparation time: 20 minutes   Cooking time: 10 minutes

Method:

1. Put all ingredients into a bowl and mix well together.
2. Turn onto a floured board or worktable, knead and roll out.
3. Using a tea cup, cut out 8 or 9 rounds.

4. Melt the butter or margarine on a heavy frying pan and fry until golden brown on each side.
5. Serve hot with plenty of extra butter.

POTATO CAKES

Potato cakes are a tasty way of using cooked leftover potatoes. They are often served at the six o'clock evening tea; Irish country people usually call it supper.

Ingredients: Serves: 4–6

8 oz mashed potatoes	**225 g**	1 cup
2 oz plain flour	**50 g**	½ cup
pinch of salt		
pinch of baking powder		
1 oz melted butter or margarine	**25 g**	1½ tbsp.
1 beaten egg		
butter or margarine for frying		
finely chopped parsley		

Preparation time: 15 minutes   Cooking time: 10–15 minutes

Method:

1. Put all ingredients into a bowl and mix well together.
2. Turn onto a floured board and knead.
3. Roll out into a circle a quarter of an inch in thickness. Gut into

8 triangles.
4. Heat butter or margarine in a frying pan and fry cakes until brown on both sides.
5. Serve hot, garnished with parley.

WHIPPED POTATOES

In times past nearly all Irish country people, even small cottiers, had a potato plot on their land. In October the potatoes not used in the summer or early autumn were dug out of the earth and stored in a shed. They softened into the spring, when they were often served whipped.

Ingredients: **Serves: 4**

1 lb potatoes	**500 g**	2 cups
seasoning		
1 oz butter	**25 g**	1½ tbsp.
¼ pint milk	**150 ml**	½ cup

Preparation time: 15 minutes   **Cooking time:** 25–35 minutes

Method:

1. Wash and peel potatoes, put into a saucepan of cold salted water, cover, bring to the boil and simmer 25 to 35 minutes (depending on size) until cooked.
2. Sieve potatoes.
3. Put butter and milk into a saucepan and bring to the boil. Add potatoes and whip well together with a wooden spoon.
4. Add nutmeg and season to taste.
5. Put into serving dish.
6. Serve hot.

COTTAGE POTATOES

These are grated potatoes, with a finely chopped raw onion added before the potatoes are cooked.

Ingredients: **Serves: 4**

1 lb potatoes	**500 g**	2 cups
2 finely chopped onions		
salt and pepper		
2 oz butter or margarine	**50 g**	¼ cup
a little milk		

Preparation time: 20 minutes   **Cooking time:** 1 hour
Oven position: centre   **Oven temperature:**
gas 6, 200°C, 400°F

Method:

1. Peel and grate potatoes, put into cold salted water for a few minutes; drain off water.
2. Add onion and season to taste.
3. Heat butter or margarine and milk in a saucepan.
4. Mix all the ingredients together and put into an ovenproof dish, put into oven for one hour.
5. Serve hot.

ROAST POTATOES

There was always plenty of fat—dripping it was called—in a country kitchen. Most people killed their own animals and rendered the fat down to liquid form. Each kind was poured into a crock and stored for weeks as a solid block. One use for the fat was in baking potatoes.

Roast potatoes are, of course, not really roasted but baked—baked in the oven in hot fat.

Ingredients: | **Serves: 4**

1 lb potatoes   **500 g**   2 cups
salt
8 oz lard for frying   **250 g**   1 cup

Preparation time: 15 minutes   **Cooking time:** stovetop: 20
Oven position: top   minutes oven: 25 minutes
Oven temperature: gas 6, 200°C, 400°F

Method:

1. Scrub and peel potatoes and put into a saucepan of cold salted water. Cover and bring to the boil, then simmer for 20 minutes.
2. Put lard into deep roasting tin and set the potatoes into the hot fat. Place tin in the oven for 25 minutes.
3. When roasted turn potatoes onto a double sheet of brown or kitchen paper and shake to remove grease.
4. Put into serving dish and serve hot.

SAVOURY BAKED POTATOES

These are baked potatoes topped with a sauce—very good as a supper dish.

Ingredients: | **Serves: 4**

4 even-sized potatoes
2 hard-boiled eggs
¼ pint mayonnaise   **150 ml**   ½ cup
2 teaspoons finely chopped parsley
2 finely chopped tomatoes
2–3 tablespoons cooked peas
seasoning

Preparation time: 15 minutes   **Cooking time:** 1 hour
Oven position: top   **Oven temperature:** gas 6, 200°C, 400°F

Method for potatoes:

1. Wash and scrub skins of potatoes, make a cross on top of each potato with a knife.
2. Arrange on a baking sheet and put into the oven for an hour.
3. When they're baked, push the pulp on each potato up slightly through the cross. Arrange on a serving dish.

Method for filling:

1. Separate the yolk from white of egg, then put yolk through a sieve and set it aside.
2. Put the egg white, mayonnaise, parsley, tomatoes and cooked peas into a bowl. Season to taste and mix well together.
3. Divide the mixture evenly between the potatoes and pile on top of each potato.
4. Sprinkle the sieved yolks over the potatoes and serve hot.

HOT POTATO SALAD

A good way of using the fine new potatoes that mature in Ireland in early summer: especially good for supper on a chilly night.

Ingredients: Serves: 4

1 lb new potatoes (small size) 8-9   **500 g**
6-8 scallions
¼ pint mayonnaise   **150 ml**   ½ cup
1 teaspoon finely chopped parsley
salt and black pepper

Preparation time: 20 minutes   **Cooking time:** 25-30 minutes

Method:

1. Peel and wash the potatoes. Boil or steam until cooked.
2. Finely chop the scallions (greens included).
3. Mix mayonnaise, scallions, parsley, salt and black pepper together.
4. Place half of the hot potatoes in a warm serving dish, coat with a little savoury mayonnaise, add remaining potatoes and coat completely with remaining savoury mayonnaise.
5. Serve hot.

BEST CHIPS

The secret of good chips—the Americans call them French fries, the French simply fried potatoes—is double dipping in hot oil made slightly hotter for the second dipping.

Ingredients: Serves: 4

4-5 large potatoes   **500 g**
good quality cooking oil

Preparation time: 20 minutes   **Cooking time:** 10-15 minutes

Method:

1. Peel potatoes and slice with potato slicer. Or use a sharp knife and cut into lengths three inches by half an inch.
2. If there's time, steep the chips in cold water to reduce the starch content.
3. Dry them well in a clean cloth or towel.
4. Fill the heavy saucepan one-third full of oil.
5. Heat the oil until it reaches 375°F. If there's no thermometer, check temperature by dropping a cube of bread into the hot oil; if it browns within one minute the temperature is right for chips.
6. Put chips into basket and gently lower them into the hot oil. (If the oil erupts violently, take the pan off the heat for a few

moments.)

7. Fry chips for four to five minutes.

8. Lift chip basket out of the oil and hang basket on lip of pot, or remove from the pot entirely. The temperature of the oil will have dropped at this stage and it is essential to reheat to about 390° F for final browning.

9. Lower basket of chips back into the reheated (and hotter) oil for one to two minutes. They should be golden brown.

10. Drain on kitchen paper, and serve hot.

OLD FASHIONED CHIPS

The French would call these sautéed potatoes. Our forebears called them chips. They were a staple for schoolchildren and at suppertime in the evening for adults.

The Irish eat potatoes every day and tend to cook more than are required for the main meal, so there are plenty left for tea. Leftover potatoes are peeled and piled onto a plate until ready to use. These sliced cooked potatoes are put onto a big, heavy frying pan with enough dripping to cover the bottom, and served with plenty of salt and pepper, or with vinegar.

Ingredients: Serves: 4

1 lb potatoes   **500 g**
1 tablespoon oil
1½ oz butter or margarine   **50 g**   2 tbsp.
salt and pepper
finely chopped parsley

Preparation time: 20 minutes   Cooking time: 30–40 minutes

Method:

1. Scrub and boil the potatoes in their skins.
2. Drain and return to their hot pan and cover (leave over gentle heat).
3. Warm oil in a frying pan, over a gentle heat.
4. Peel and slice the potatoes, return them to the hot dry pan and cover them up.
5. Add the butter or margarine to the frying pan (to prevent burning and spitting) and increase heat to mixture.
6. Season to taste, add parsley, shake to remove excess fat and serve as soon as possible.

POTATO AND ONION PIE

This is a nourishing hot dish, often served at suppertime with cold meat.

Ingredients: Serves: 4–6

1 lb parboiled potatoes (5–6)   **500 g**   5–6 cups
2 oz butter or margarine   **50 g**   ¼ cup

2 thinly sliced onions
2 oz grated cheddar cheese   **50 g**   ½ cup
¼ pint milk   **150 ml**   ½ cup
salt and freshly ground black pepper

Preparation time: 20 minutes   **Cooking time:** 35 minutes
Oven position: centre   **Oven temperature:**
                                         gas 6, 200°C, 400°F

Method:

1. Slice the parboiled potatoes.
2. Heat the fat in a pan and lightly fry the onions over a gentle heat without browning for a minute.
3. Put a layer of sliced potatoes into the bottom of a greased pie dish. Cover with a layer of onions, sprinkle a little cheese over and season lightly.
4. Continue layering the remaining ingredients, keeping back some grated cheese.
5. Pour milk over and sprinkle grated cheese on top.
6. Place in the oven and cook until there is a nice golden colour on top.

VEGETABLES IN A SHELL

People can become confused about the tomato. Some cookbooks list it as a vegetable; others as a fruit. What the tomato is in fact is a very versatile fruit served and eaten as a vegetable. Irish tomatoes are of superior flavour and taste.

The following is basically a tomato dish, with the tomatoes used both for their pulp and as shells for the savoury filling.

Ingredients: **Serves: 6–8**

6–8 large firm tomatoes
3–4 medium-sized cooked potatoes (mashed)
3–4 finely chopped scallions
1 tablespoon oil
1 teaspoon vinegar
1 teaspoon finely chopped basil
salt and black pepper

Preparation time: 20 minutes   **Cooking time:** 20 minutes
Oven position: centre   **Oven temperature:**
                                         gas 6, 200°C, 400°F

Method:

1. Cut a slice (or cap) from the rounded side of each tomato, remove the pulp carefully.
2. Put the pulp through a sieve.
3. Put the potatoes into a bowl.
4. Take a fork and beat together the scallions and tomato pulp along with the oil, vinegar, basil

and seasoning.

5. Add this to the potatoes and mix well together.
6. Place tomatoes on a baking sheet and pile filling into tomato shells.
7. Put cap on each tomato and set into the oven.
8. Serve hot either as an appetizer or with the main course.

TOMATOES IN SOUR CREAM

Ingredients: Serves: 6

6 medium-sized tomatoes
1 finely chopped onion
salt and black pepper
2 oz butter   **50 g**   ¼ cup
¼ pint sour cream   **150 ml**   ½ cup
finely chopped parsley

Preparation time: 10 minutes   **Cooking time:** 8 minutes

Method:

1. Cut the tomatoes into thick slices and season with salt and pepper.
2. Melt butter in a frying pan and fry the onion until it is transparent.
3. Add tomatoes, cook over a gentle heat for three or four minutes.
4. Stir in sour cream; beat thoroughly over a gentle heat for a minute.
5. Arrange on a serving dish and garnish with parsley.

DRESSED MUSHROOMS

There are two main types of mushrooms in Ireland, the wild mushrooms—flat and open, with far better flavour—and the capped or button-shaped cultivated mushrooms.

Ingredients: Serves: 4

½ lb mushrooms   **250 g**   2 cups
juice and rind of a lemon
¼ pint yoghurt   **150 ml**   ½ cup
1 teaspoon finely chopped parsley
seasoning

Preparation time: 15 minutes   **Cooking time:** 5 minutes

Method:

1. Clean mushrooms by rubbing with a damp cloth and a little salt; then slice them.
2. Put mushrooms, juice and rind of lemon into a saucepan, cover and place over a gentle heat and cook for five minutes.
3. Remove from the heat, put into

serving dish; add yoghurt, chopped parsley and season to taste; mix well together.

4. Serve cold.

STUFFED CABBAGE ROLLS

The cabbage is a vegetable long established in Ireland. There are several varieties available: spring cabbage, winter cabbage, white cabbage and red cabbage.

Ingredients: Serves: 4–6

1 head cabbage		
1 oz butter or margarine	**25 g**	1½ tbsp.
1 oz flour	**25 g**	¼ cup
¼ pint milk	**150 ml**	½ cup
4 oz cooked rice	**100 g**	2 cups
4 oz cooked chopped meat	**100 g**	⅔ cup
1 diced onion		
1 crushed clove garlic		
seasoning		
¼ pint stock	**150 ml**	½ cup

Preparation time: 20 minutes
Oven position: centre

Cooking time: 25 minutes
Oven temperature:
gas 5, 190°C, 375°F

Method:

1. Prepare cabbage: cut into four, remove stumps, wash each leaf in cold salted water.
2. Blanch by putting in boiling salted water for 1 or 2 minutes.
3. Melt margarine or butter, add the flour and blend well together, cook for one minute. Gradually add the milk and bring to the boil.
4. Add the rice, cooked meat, onion and garlic, and season to taste.
5. Fill the cabbage leaves with the stuffing and roll up.
6. Put into a casserole dish and pour stock into casserole. Place in the oven.
7. Using a spatula, transfer stuffed rolls onto a serving plate. Serve hot.

Watchpoints:

Spring cabbage is tender and green with a shining smooth leaf. Winter cabbage is green with a firm texture and a curly leaf. It is tougher than spring cabbage and requires a little longer time in cooking. White cabbage is very firm and keeps well. It is served either cooked or uncooked. Shredded finely, it's used a lot in coleslaw. Red cabbage is a dark red cabbage, used like white cabbage and is particularly good for pickling.

CAULIFOWER IN ALL ITS GLORY

Cauliflower consists of tiny white florets formed into a large compact head. It can be cooked whole and then broken back into the florets. It is often presented dressed with a white sauce sprinkled with cheese or breadcrumbs. Below is one of the best ways of serving it.

Ingredients:　　　　　　　　　　　　Serves: 4

1 cauliflower		
seasoning		
1 oz butter or margarine	25 g	1½ tbsp.
1 oz flour	25 g	¼ cup
¾ pint milk	425 ml	2 cups
2 oz chopped almonds	50 g	⅓ cup
egg yolk sieved		
finely chopped parsley		

Preparation time: 20 minutes　　**Cooking time:** 30 minutes

Method:

1. Cut cauliflower into 4 to 6 pieces and cook in salted boiling water until tender.
2. Put the cauliflower into a bowl with heads arranged downwards. The bowl should only be big enough to hold the cauliflower). Keep warm.
3. Meantime, melt the margarine or butter, add the flour and cook for a minute.
4. Gradually add the liquid, bring to the boil, season to taste, and add the chopped almonds.
5. Upturn bowl on a small serving dish so that florets are set upwards.
6. Garnish cauliflower with sieved egg yolk and parsley.
7. Spoon a little sauce over cauliflower. Pour remaining sauce into a sauce boat and serve hot.

FRIED LEEKS AND BACON

Because of their much more delicate flavour leeks make a dish acceptable even to many who dislike onions.

Ingredients:　　　　　　　　　　　　Serves: 4–6

6 oz chopped streaky bacon	175 g	1 cup
3–4 tablespoons oil		
1 lb leeks	500 g	3–4 leeks
2 chopped onions		
seasoning		

Preparation time: 15 minutes　　**Cooking time:** 25 minutes

Method:

1. Blanch the bacon by putting it into cold water and bring it to the boil. Strain off liquid.
2. Heat the oil in a deep heavy pan. Add bacon, leeks and onions, and season to taste.
3. Cover and simmer for 25 minutes.
4. Serve hot.

STUFFED VEGETABLE MARROW

The young vegetable marrow is best: the skin is tender and the seed is hardly formed. It has a dark green outer skin with delicate flesh inside. It is usually fried in slices or—as here—stuffed and baked.

Ingredients: Serves: 6

1 small marrow		
2 oz butter or margarine	50 g	¼ cup
2 finely chopped onions		
1 seeded and chopped green pepper		
4 oz breadcrumbs	100 g	2 cups
3 tomatoes (chopped, seeded and skinned)		
seasoning		

Preparation time: 15 minutes   **Cooking time:** 45–50 minutes
Oven position: centre   **Oven temperature:**
gas 5, 190°C, 375°F

Method:

1. Cut the marrow into half-inch slices and put into a greased ovenproof dish.
2. Melt the butter or margarine and lightly fry the onions and pepper.
3. Add the breadcrumbs and tomatoes; mix well together. Season to taste.
4. Divide the stuffing evenly between slices of marrow.
5. Cover casserole and place in oven.
6. Serve hot.

BUTTERED CELERY

This long-stemmed, crisp watery vegetable is often used to decorate a buffet table. It can be dipped in savoury sauce and eaten raw. But I like it cooked in plenty of butter, as in this recipe.

Ingredients: Serves: 4–6

1 head celery		
2 oz butter	50 g	¼ cup
salt and freshly ground pepper		

Preparation time: 10 minutes   **Cooking time:** 30 minutes
Oven position: top   **Oven temperature:** gas 6, 200°C, 400°F

Method:

1. Remove the green tops from the celery. Break the sticks away from the roots; wash well in cold salted water.
2. Cut each stalk into four.
3. Heat the butter in an ovenproof dish; put in the celery and season to taste, cover and place in the oven until tender—about 30 minutes.
4. Serve hot.

VEGETABLE HOTPOT

Irish people did not always have meat readily available: but the lack of meat did not mean they starved. They made good meals out of the vegetables they grew themselves.

The vegetables were cooked together in a saucepan, thickened with blended flour, served up on large plates, and generally eaten with a large spoon, like colcannon. Here is one variation on a most basic Irish vegetable recipe.

Ingredients: Serves: 6–8

2 sliced courgettes
1 seeded and sliced green or red
    pepper
4 seeded and sliced tomatoes
2 sliced onions
2 teaspoons finely chopped parsley
seasoning
1 seeded and sliced aubergine
1 crushed clove of garlic
1 tablespoon oil
1 pint vegetable soup   **575 ml**   2$\frac{1}{2}$ cups
4 oz peas   **100 g** $\frac{2}{3}$ cups
12 oz cooked mashed potatoes **350 g**   1$\frac{1}{2}$ cups
seasoning

Preparation time: 25 minutes   **Cooking time:** 40 minutes

Method:

1. Prepare vegetables.
2. Heat oil in a large saucepan, gently fry vegetables except for peas, potatoes and parsley.
3. Add the soup and parsley to the fried vegetables, bring to the boil; cover and simmer for 30–35 minutes.
4. Add peas and potatoes, bring to the boil and continue cooking for a further 10 minutes.
5. Season to taste and serve hot.

BUTTERED CARROTS

Carrots are available in Ireland all year round; young carrots come in the springtime. The young ones make tastier eating but old carrots are best for stocks and sauces.

Ingredients: **Serves: 4–6**

1 lb washed and scraped carrots	**500 g**	7–8 carrots
1 oz butter	**25 g**	1½ tbsp.
cold water		
salt and pepper		
2 teaspoons finely chopped parsley		
1 oz melted butter	**25 g**	1½ tbsp.

Preparation time: 15 minutes **Cooking time:** 25 minutes

Method:

1. Put carrots into saucepan with butter and just enough cold water to barely cover them. Add seasoning.
2. Cook with the lid on until tender.
3. Remove lid and continue cooking until all the water has evaporated.
4. Add parsley, check seasoning and serve hot in heated serving dish, sprinkle with chopped parsley.

CARROT AND PARSNIP MASH

During the harvest at home we washed and scrubbed the carrots and parsnips in the water tank at the bottom of the yard. We'd put the clean parsnips back into the water and watch them float.

Parsnips have a beautiful delicate flavour and can be cooked in several different ways. One way is to cook carrots and parsnips together, mash and season them well and serve them with plenty of butter, as in this recipe.

Ingredients: **Serves: 8–10**

1 lb small carrots	**500 g**	7–8 carrots
1 lb new parsnips	**500 g**	7–8 parsnips
seasoning		
3 oz butter	**75 g**	⅓ cup

Preparation time: 10 minutes **Cooking time:** 10–15 minutes

Method:

1. Scrape, wash and slice the vegetables.
2. Put vegetables into saucepan, barely covering them with cold water; add a little seasoning and 1 tablespoon of butter and cover. Bring to the boil. Reduce heat and simmer about 10 minutes until tender.
3. When tender, all the water will have evaporated.
4. Mash vegetables, add remaining butter, check taste of seasoning.
5. Put into serving dish and serve hot.

115

CREAMY SWEDES

Swedes are members of the turnip family—called 'mitabaga' in the U.S.—they are large firm vegetables which have a strong flavour when cooked.

Ingredients: **Serves: 4–6**

1 turnip
2 oz butter or margarine   **50 g**   ¼ cup
seasoning

Preparation time: 10 minutes   **Cooking time:** 15–20 minutes

Method:

1. Peel the turnip: a coarse, thick skin will come off.
2. Slice and put into cold salted water.
3. Bring to the boil and cook for 15 to 20 minutes until just tender (avoid overcooking).
4. Drain and mash.
5. Melt the butter and add the mashed turnip. Season to taste.
6. Pile into serving dish and serve hot.

CROWNED BEETROOT

Beets are a wine-coloured root vegetable. Small beets have a better flavour and texture than very large ones. Beetroot is generally served cold in a salad. But it can be very tasty heated or served with a hot dish as here.

Ingredients: **Serves: 6**

6 large slices beetroot
12 oz boiled potatoes   **325 g**   4–5 potatoes
1 oz butter   **25 g**   1½ tbsp.
2 tablespoons milk
seasoning
3 hard-boiled eggs
3 tablespoons mayonnaise
1–2 teaspoons chopped parsley
2 oz grated cheese   **50 g**   ½ cup

Preparation time: 20 minutes

Method:

1. Place the 6 beet slices on a serving dish.
2. Mash the potatoes. Melt the butter, add milk and bring to the boil. Then add mashed potatoes, season to taste and beat well together.
3. Put potatoes into pastry bag and pipe a border of potatoes around the edge of each slice of

116

beet.

4. Cut eggs in half on the width, remove the yolks and put through a sieve.
5. Mix sieved yolks, mayonnaise, and chopped parsley together and season to taste. Pipe mixture into the egg white.
6. Stand each filled egg white in the centre within the potato border.
7. Sprinkle with grated cheese and serve.

WEIGHTS AND MEASURES

An important point to remember with regard to solid measures. Irish cooks are generous with their teaspoon and tablespoon measures: these are usually heaped, while the American cook levels off the quantity on the spoon with a knife. So it is important to note that where a recipe specifies a teaspoon of sugar, for example, you should use a rounded teaspoonful, i.e. as much above the spoon as in it, or **two** level teaspoonfuls.

Sauces

In years past the Irish weren't much interested in sauces. They were satisfied to cook their meat and vegetables together in water, and to serve the liquid left over from the cooking as a sort of sauce. When roast meat was served some fat from the pan was poured over the meat and vegetables, and this was sauce enough. White sauces were made by boiling milk and adding blended cornflour to thicken it. Seasoned with salt and pepper, this was a savoury sauce. Or sugar was added to make it a sweet white sauce, which was generally served with stewed fruit or jam on top.

Today, however, Irish cooks are very much aware of all the range of sauces available for use with different cuts of meat and vegetables. They pride themselves on making the tastiest dishes they can manage.

Many sauces take little more than five or ten minutes to prepare.

WHITE SAUCES

White sauces are the most basic, the variation in the first four following is in the amount of milk.

Method for all white sauces:

1. Melt the margarine or butter; add the flour and stir with a wooden spoon over a gentle heat for a minute or so.
2. Gradually add the milk, then bring to the boil and season to taste, stirring continuously.
3. Simmer for 5 minutes.
4. Pour into a sauceboat and serve hot.

POURING SAUCE

Ingredients:

1 oz butter or margarine	**25 g**	1½ tbsp.
1 oz flour	**25 g**	¼ cup
1 pint milk	**575 ml**	2½ cups
seasoning		

STEWING SAUCE

Ingredients:

1 oz butter or margarine	**25 g**	1½ tbsp.
1 oz flour	**25 g**	¼ cup
¾ pint milk	**425 ml**	2 cups
seasoning		

COATING SAUCE
Ingredients:

1 oz butter or margarine	25 g	1½ tbsp.
1 oz flour	25 g	¼ cup
½ pint milk	275 ml	1¼ cup
seasoning		

PARNARD SAUCE
Ingredients:

1 oz butter or margarine	25 g	1½ tbsp.
1 oz flour	25 g	¼ cup
¼ pint liquid	150 ml	½ cup
seasoning		

PARSLEY SAUCE
Add 1 tablespoon finely chopped parsley to basic stewing sauce.

ONION SAUCE
Add one medium-sized chopped onion to pouring sauce.

CAPER SAUCE
Add one tablespoon chopped capers to pouring sauce.

CHEESE SAUCE
2 oz grated cheese (50 g; ½ cup), a shake of cayenne pepper and a teaspoon of mustard to basic stewing sauce.

MUSTARD SAUCE
Add one tablespoon mustard and one tablespoon vinegar to basic stewing sauce.

For sauces that follow, the methods vary a bit.

BECHAMEL SAUCE
Ingredients:

6–8 cloves		
1 onion		
1 bay leaf		
a blade of mace		
½ pint milk	275 ml	1¼ cups
1 oz margarine	25 g	1½ tbsp.
1 oz flour	25 g	¼ cup
seasoning		

Method:
1. Press cloves into the onion.
2. Put the onion, bayleaf, mace and milk into a saucepan. Cover and simmer gently for 20 min-utes. Bring to the boil and strain off flavoured milk.
3. Continue as for white sauce, using flavoured milk.

BREAD SAUCE
Ingredients:

6–8 cloves
1 medium-sized onion
½ pint milk   **275 ml**   1¼ cups
3 oz breadcrumbs   **75 g**   1½ cups
seasoning

Method:
1. Stick cloves into the peeled onion, put into a saucepan with the milk and simmer in the milk for 30 minutes over a gentle heat.
2. Remove onion and cloves, add breadcrumbs and seasoning, simmer for 10 minutes.

HORSERADISH SAUCE
Ingredients:

2 tablespoons grated horseradish
1 teaspoon sugar
seasoning
1 tablespoon vinegar
1 teaspoon lemon juice
1 tablespoon milk

Method:
1. Mix all ingredients together. Extra milk may be added to give a thinner consistency.

HOLLANDAISE SAUCE
Ingredients:

3 tablespoons wine vinegar
a few peppercorns
a blade of mace
3 oz butter   **75 g**   ⅓ cup
2 egg yolks

Method:
1. Put vinegar, peppercorns and mace into a saucepan over a strong heat; boil to reduce to 1 tablespoon and strain.

2. Soften the butter by working it with a wooden spoon.
3. Cream the egg yolks in a small bowl with a knob of butter, mix in strained vinegar; set the bowl in a saucepan half filled with hot water over a gentle heat.
4. Continue beating sauce with a wooden spoon, adding knobs of butter until thick.

TOMATO SAUCE

Ingredients:

1 oz butter or margarine	25 g	1½ tbsp.
4 oz chopped onion	100 g	1 cup
4 large tomatoes (seeded, skinned, and chopped)		
1 oz flour	25 g	¼ cup
¼ pint milk	150 ml	½ cup
¼ pint stock	150 ml	½ cup
1 teaspoon sugar		
bouquet garni		
seasoning		

Method:
1. Heat butter or margarine and gently fry the onion.
2. Add the tomatoes and flour, then cook for a minute.
3. Gradually add the milk, stock, sugar, bouquet garni, stirring continuously and bring to the boil; season to taste.
4. Simmer for 10 minutes.
5. Strain and serve hot.

MINT SAUCE

Ingredients:

Fresh mint leaves
1 tablespoon fine sugar
1 tablespoon vinegar
hot water

Method:
1. Chop mint leaves, sprinkle with a little sugar.
2. Put into a sauceboat, add vinegar and just cover with hot water.
3. Leave to stand at least 20 minutes before serving.

CURRY SAUCE

Ingredients:

1½ oz margarine	50 g	2 tbsp.
1 chopped onion		
1 seeded and chopped red or		

green pepper
1 oz flour   **25 g**   ¼ cup
1 teaspoon curry powder
   (depending on strength)
1 chopped tomato
1 cored and chopped apple
¾ pint stock   **500 ml**   2 cups

Method:
1. Melt the margarine, gently fry the onion and pepper; add flour and curry powder, and cook thoroughly for one or two minutes.
2. Add the tomato and apple.
3. Gradually add the stock, bring to the boil.
4. Cover and leave to simmer over a gentle heat for 40 to 45 minutes.

BROWN SAUCE
Ingredients:

1 oz margarine   **25 g**   1½ tbsp.
1 oz flour   **25 g**   ¼ cup
¾ pint stock   **500 ml**   2 cups
seasoning

Method:
1. Melt the margarine, add the flour and beat with a metal spoon; continue cooking for one or two minutes until the flour is a rich brown colour, stirring continuously.
2. Add the stock gradually, bring to the boil and season to taste.

BROWN GRAVY
Ingredients:

roasting joint
1 teaspoon finely chopped herbs
1 roughly chopped onion
1 tablespoon flour   **25 g**   ¼ cup
½ pint stock   **275 ml**   1¼ cups

Method:
1. Add herbs and onions to roasting tin 15 minutes before joint is finished cooking.
2. Remove roasting joint and tip off all but 1 tablespoon of meat juice.
3. Add flour, blend in with metal spoon for one or two minutes until brown.
4. Add liquid gradually, bring to the boil, season to taste and strain into a sauceboat.

ORANGE SAUCE

Ingredients:

1 whole orange cut into segments
2 oz butter or margarine   **50 g**   ¼ cup
rind and juice of 1 orange
2 oz brown sugar   **50 g**   ¼ cup

Method:

1. Fry orange segments, grated rind and sugar in the melted butter or margarine for three or four minutes over a gentle heat until golden brown.
2. Add orange juice, bring to the boil, simmer until syrupy.

APPLE SAUCE

Ingredients:

4 medium apples
1 tablespoon water
nutmeg
1 tablespoon cream (optional)

Method:

1. Peel, core and slice apples.
2. Put into a saucepan with water and nutmeg; cook slowly for five to seven minutes over a gentle heat, until tender.
3. Beat the apples and put through a sieve.
4. If using cream, allow sauce to cool and fold it into apples.

SOUR CREAM SAUCE

Ingredients:

½ pint sour cream   **275 ml**   1¼ cups
1 teaspoon bottled horseradish
2 scallions finely chopped
  (including greens)
seasoning

Method:

1. Combine ingredients well together.
2. Put into sauceboat.
3. Serve with cold meats, fish or vegetables.

THICK MAYONNAISE

Ingredients:

3 egg yolks

a pinch of salt and pepper
a pinch of dry mustard
1 tablespoon white wine vinegar or
    lemon juice
½ pint oil   **275 ml**   1¼ cups
1 tablespoon whipped cream

Method:
1. Cream the yolks with salt, pepper, mustard and vinegar in a bowl.
2. Add the oil very gradually, beating continuously until thick.
3. Fold in the cream.

EGG DRESSING

Ingredients:

¼ pint yoghurt   **150 ml**   ½ cup
1 tablespoon mayonnaise
1 tablespoon whipped cream
hard-boiled eggs
cayenne pepper

Method:
1. Mix yoghurt, mayonnaise and whipped cream together.
2. Coat sliced hard-boiled eggs with dressing.
3. Dredge lightly with cayenne pepper.

SALAD DRESSING

Ingredients:

3 tablespoons oil
1 tablespoon vinegar
seasoning
1 teaspoon finely chopped fresh herbs

Method:
1. Put all ingredients into a bowl and blend well together.

WHISKEY SAUCE

Ingredients:

1 oz cornflour   **25 g**   1½ tbsp.
1 oz caster sugar   **25 g**   1½ tbsp.
¾ pint milk   **425 ml**   2 cups
2–3 tablespoons Irish whiskey

Method:
1. Blend the cornflour with a little milk.
2. Put the remaining milk on to heat.
3. Add the blended cornflour to the heated milk.
4. Bring to the boil, simmer for four to five minutes, add sugar and whiskey.

CUSTARD SAUCE

Ingredients:

2 teaspoons cornflour		
1 pint milk	575 ml	2½ cups
1-2 egg yolks		
a few drops of vanilla essence		
1 oz caster sugar	25 g	1½ tbsp.

Method:
1. Blend cornflour with a little milk; put remaining milk on to heat.
2. Cream the yolks, cornflour, vanilla essence and sugar together in a bowl.
3. Pour the heated milk into the bowl, stirring continuously. Rinse the saucepan in cold water; pour the liquid back into the saucepan, and cook for three to four minutes over a gentle heat stirring continuously, but do not boil.

ALMOND CREAM SAUCE

Ingredients:

1 oz cornflour	25 g	¼ cup
2 egg yolks		
¾ pint milk	450 ml	2 cups
1 oz caster sugar	25 g	1½ tbsp.
3 oz ground almonds	75 g	½ cup
a few drops of almond essence		

Method:
1. Blend cornflour with egg yolks and a little milk.
2. Put remaining milk into a saucepan and heat almost to boiling point.
3. Pour the heated milk onto the egg yolks and cornflour, stirring continuously. Rinse saucepan in cold water.
4. Pour liquid back into the saucepan; add sugar, ground almonds and almond essence.
5. Bring to boiling point over a gentle heat, stirring continuously but do not boil.

RICH PASTRY CREAM

Ingredients:

1½ oz cornflour	**40 g**	⅓ cup
2 egg yolks		
1 pint milk	**575 ml**	2½ cups
2 oz caster sugar	**50 g**	¼ cup
1 oz butter	**25 g**	1½ tbsp.
flavouring		

Method:

1. Prepare as for almond cream sauce, adding the butter instead of almond, and mix in with the granulated sugar.

CHOCOLATE SAUCE

Ingredients:

8 oz cooking chocolate	**225 g**	8 squares
(sweet chocolate)		
a knob of butter		
5–6 tablespoons milk		

Method:

1. Put the chocolate into a bowl and stand it in a saucepan half filled with hot water. Set saucepan over a gentle heat until the chocolate has melted.
2. Mix in the butter and stir in the ·milk; beat together with a wooden spoon.

JAM SAUCE

Ingredients:

3 tablespoons jam		¼ cup
¼ pint water	**150 ml**	½ cup
1 teaspoon arrowroot		

Method:

1. Put jam and water into a saucepan. Bring gently to the boil.
2. Blend arrowroot with 2 tablespoons water.
3. Remove from the heat, add the blended arrowroot, stirring continuously; return to the heat and re-boil.

Salads

Ireland's damp chilly climate is perhaps one reason why the Irish used to make so little of salads. Cold meat, a few leaves of lettuce, a bit of beetroot, egg and tomato: that was the Irish salad, little bother with sauces or dressings. Today formal salads have become popular, and are served as appetizers, as meals in themselves, and as side dishes to a main course; and fresh fruit salads are served as desserts.

GREEN SALAD

Ingredients: **Serves: 4–6**

1 clove garlic (with skin removed)
1 head lettuce
6 sticks celery
1 tablespoon chopped parsley
½ cucumber
4–6 scallions
salad dressing

Preparation time: 15 minutes

Method:
1. Rub the garlic around sides and base of the salad bowl.
2. Wash and drain lettuce, celery and parsley (remove any discoloured leaves).
3. Cut celery into one-inch pieces and thin-slice the cucumber.
4. Top and tail the scallions, remove outer skin from root, cut into one-inch lengths.
5. Arrange salad in bowl. Toss it with salad dressing just before serving.

ASPARAGUS SALAD

Ingredients: **Serves: 4–6**

2 bunches asparagus
2 oz Irish blue cheese   **50 g**   ⅓ cup
salad dressing
finely chopped parsley

Preparation time: 15 minutes   **Cooking time:** 10–15 minutes

Method:
1. Wash asparagus, leave whole; cook covered in boiling salted water.
2. Blend the cheese into the salad dressing.

3. Arrange the cooked asparagus on a serving dish.
4. Pour dressing over the asparagus (avoid pouring dressing over heads).
5. Garnish with chopped parsley.

EGG AND BEAN SALAD

Ingredients: Serves: 4–6

6 sliced hard-boiled eggs
1 lb cooked long green beans   **500 g**   4 cups
½ pint yoghurt   **275 ml**   1¼ cups
1–2 tablespoons lightly whipped
  cream
seasoning
paprika

Preparation time: 20 minutes

Method:

1. Arrange a single line of overlapping egg slices down the centre of an oval-shaped dish.
2. Place the beans on either side and finish with a border of overlapping egg slices.
3. Mix yoghurt, cream and seasoning well together, and pour over the eggs.
4. Sprinkle lightly with paprika.

FISH SALAD

Ingredients: Serves: 6

6 fillets of sole
juice of a half lemon
1 oz butter or margarine   **25 g**   1½ tbsp.
seasoning
1 lb cooked baby carrots   **500 g**   7–8 carrots
1 lb cooked new potatoes   **500 g**   4–5 potatoes
1 teaspoon finely chopped parsley
½ pint yoghurt   **275 ml**   1¼ cups
a few wedges of lemon

Preparation time: 25 minutes   **Cooking time:** 20 minutes
Oven position: centre   **Oven temperature:**
                                          gas 6, 200°C, 400°F

Method:

1. Wash and roll up each fillet of sole.
2. Place in a greased ovenproof dish and pour lemon juice onto fish; dot with knobs of margarine and season to taste.
3. Cover with a buttered sheet of greaseproof or brown paper and bake for 20 minutes.
4. Allow to cool.

5. Arrange fish surrounded by carrots in centre of serving dish.
6. If potatoes are large, cut in two and arrange around the edge of dish. Sprinkle with chopped parsley.
7. Pour yoghurt over the fish and garnish with lemon wedges.

CHICKEN SALAD

Ingredients: Serves: 4

1 lb cooked chicken	500 g	2 cups
6–8 radishes		
6–8 lettuce leaves		
seasoning		
4 tablespoons mayonnaise		½ cup
2 tablespoons Irish blue cheese		⅓ cup
2 oz cooked peas	50 g	¼ cup
salad dressing		

Preparation time: 25 minutes

Method:
1. Dice the chicken.
2. Top and tail radishes, wash well and slice.
3. Wash lettuce leaves, dry well and arrange in salad bowl.
4. Season chicken and arrange it in the centre of lettuce.
5. Blend the mayonnaise and cheese together and then pour over the chicken.
6. Decorate with radishes and peas.
7. Pour a little salad dressing over the lettuce just before serving.

APPLE AND SAUSAGE SALAD

This is one of my favourite salads, and a good item for the buffet table. Chopped raw celery adds a welcome crispness.

Ingredients: Serves: 4–6

1 lb sausages	500 g	
1 lb dessert apples	500 g	4–5 apples
seasoning		
½ pint mayonnaise or salad cream	275 ml	1¼ cups
1 grated carrot		

Preparation time: 20 minutes   **Cooking time:** 10 minutes

Method:
1. Grill sausages and cut into one-inch pieces.
2. Peel, core and slice apples.
3. Mix apples and sausage together and season to taste.
4. Pour in mayonnaise and mix well.
5. Arrange in salad bowl and sprinkle with grated carrot.

ORANGE AND LIVER SALAD

This is nice as a lunch or supper dish. Liver has a close texture, but when it is combined with fresh fruit and well seasoned, it can be very appetizing. To make it even more attractive, it can be served in the fruit shell.

Ingredients:

2 large oranges		
8 oz cooked liver	**250 g**	1 cup
1 finely chopped shallot		
or 1 small onion		
2 oz breadcrumbs	**50 g**	1 cup
1–2 tablespoons oil		
seasoning		
orange segments		

Preparation time: 20 minutes

Method:

1. Wash and dry oranges and cut in half; and remove flesh from skins carefully. Cut the flesh into segments and remove pips. Reserve orange shells.
2. Mince or finely chop the liver.
3. Blend the liver, shallot, garlic and breadcrumbs well together with the orange segments and oil; season to taste.
4. Pile into orange shells and garnish with orange segments.

HAM AND PINEAPPLE SALAD

Home cooked ham has a beautiful flavour when boiled. It is nicer still when put into a roasting tin afterwards and baked in the oven for half an hour. If it is to be baked the boiling time is cut by an hour.

This salad is one good method of using up pieces of ham left over from the carving.

Ingredients: Serves: 2–4

4 pineapple rings		
4 finely-chopped slices of ham		
1 oz grated nuts	**25 g**	¼ cup
2 oz cooked rice	**50 g**	1 cup
2 oz cooked peas	**50 g**	⅓ cup
seasoning		
salad dressing		
a few tomato wedges		

Preparation time: 20 minutes

Method:

1. Arrange pineapple rings on a serving dish.
2. Mix all the ingredients together and season to taste, pour in the salad dressing and blend well together.
3. Divide filling evenly between pineapple rings and pile into the centre of each pineapple ring.
4. Garnish with tomato wedges.

TONGUE SALAD

Ingredients: Serves: 3–4

2 hard-boiled eggs
8 oz diced, cooked tongue   **250 g**   1 cup
2 oz cooked, long-grain rice   **50 g**   1 cup
1 seeded and finely shredded
   green pepper
1 finely chopped medium-sized onion
salad dressing
seasoning

Preparation time: 25 minutes

Method:

1. Remove egg yolks from whites; put yolks through a fine sieve and set aside. Chop whites.
2. Put the tongue, rice, pepper, onion and egg white into a bowl and mix well together; add salad dressing and season to taste.
3. Pile into a salad bowl and garnish with sieved egg yolks.

STUFFED MEAT SALAD

Ingredients: Serves: 2

2–3 stalks of celery
1 apple
2 cooked sausages
mayonnaise to taste
salt and pepper
4 slices of cooked ham or beef
slices of red apple dipped in lemon juice

Preparation time: 20 minutes   **Cooking time: 10 minutes**
                                             (sausages)

Method:

1. Wash celery and cut into one-inch pieces. Wash, core and grate apple. Cut the cooked sausages into neat one-inch pieces.
2. Mix celery, apple, sausages and

131

mayonnaise together and season to taste.

3. Divide filling evenly between the slices of meat and roll up.

4. Arrange salad on an oval-shaped serving plate, and decorate with slices of apple.

COLESLAW

Coleslaw has become very popular and is served with salads, cold meats or sometimes as a salad substitute. Coleslaws can vary considerably. Usually finely shredded white cabbage, onion and carrots are seasoned well and mixed together with mayonnaise or salad cream. Shredded apples, nuts, dried fruit, and red or green peppers can be added to vary the taste and texture.

Ingredients: Serves: 4–6

½ head white cabbage
1 seeded and chopped red pepper
1 peeled and cored dessert apple
4 sticks celery
2 carrots
1 onion
seasoning
½ pint mayonnaise   **250 ml**   1¼ cups
chopped parsley

Preparation time: 20 minutes

Method:

1. Cut cabbage in half, remove outer leaves and stems, wash in cold salted water.
2. Wash and scrape celery and carrots; remove skin from onions.

3. Finely shred vegetables and fruit.
4. Season to taste and bind with mayonnaise.
5. Arrange in serving dish and garnish with parsley.

WEIGHTS AND MEASURES

An important point to remember with regard to solid measures. Irish cooks are generous with their teaspoon and tablespoon measures: these are usually heaped, while the American cook levels off the quantity on the spoon with a knife. So it is important to note that where a recipe specifies a teaspoon of sugar, for example, you should use a rounded teaspoonful, i.e. as much above the spoon as in it, or **two** level teaspoonfuls.

Pastry

Years ago shortcrust pastry meant fruit tarts or pies; richer pastries were used to cover a savoury pie. Today all kinds of pastry are popular, and used not only for pies and tarts but also for chocolate eclairs, quiche Lorraine, beef Wellington, chicken puffs and a wide variety of other dishes. Homemade pastry is far superior in flavour to readymade pastry, especially when butter is used in the making. Pastry adds to the body of a dish; it also adds to its appearance. It can be brushed over with egg or milk to give it a nice shiny surface. It can be decorated with bits of pastry shaped into leaves or even roses and its edges can be fluted or platted in various ways.

HINTS ON PASTRY MAKING

1. Use the correct amounts of ingredients given in the recipes so as to obtain the proper balance between butter, margarine or other fat on the one hand, and flour on the other.
2. A very cool airy room is most important for making good pastry, particularly the richer varieties—to avoid the pastry becoming soggy and unmanageable.
3. All pasty should be handled lightly but firmly; too much handling will produce a greasy and unmanageable pastry.
4. Never stretch pastry; it will shrink back during baking.
5. Plain flour should always be used. Using self-raising flour or adding baking powder to flour gives the pastry a spongy texture. The only exception is when cheese is added to short pastry: baking powder helps lighten it and reduces the greasiness caused by the cheese.
6. Avoid using egg white as it toughens the pastry.
7. Biscuit pastry may break when rolled out, but it can easily be patched up.
8. Use butter when possible, particularly for the richer pastry: butter gives a better flavour.
9. All pastry can be labelled and put into the freezer for storage.
10. Most pastry meat pies keep for two or three months or longer; pastry fruit pies and tarts, or unfilled pastry, for six months. Most can be frozen without first being baked.
11. Uncooked choux pastry can be made in bulk, put into a bowl, covered with cellophane, and set to rest in the refrigerator, but should be baked the following day. When freezing choux pastry, the procedure is to bake, cook, fill, freeze and wrap after freezing. Use empty choux shells within five months; if filled, within two or three months.
12. All pastry should have about half as much butter or margarine as flour by weight. There is no need to grease the plate or tin, except for choux pastry, which needs a greased tin.

SHORTCRUST PASTRY

Ingredients:

6 oz plain flour	**175 g**	1½ cups
pinch of salt		
3 oz margarine	**75 g**	⅓ cup
cold water		

Preparation time: 10 minutes

Method:

1. Sieve flour and salt into a bowl. Cut up margarine and rub into the flour with tips of fingers until the mixture resembles fine breadcrumbs.
2. Add enough cold water to make a firm dough, mixing dough with a knife.
3. Turn out onto a floured board; and knead lightly with tips of fingers.
4. Press out a little with rolling pin; roll out into desired shape with light even strokes.
5. Cover and refrigerate for an hour before using.
6. Fill and bake, following the recipe.

FLEUR PASTRY

Ingredients:

6 oz plain flour	**175 g**	1½ cups
pinch of salt		
3 oz margarine	**75 g**	⅓ cup
1 oz caster sugar	**25 g**	1½ tbsp.
1 egg yolk		
cold water		

Preparation time: 10 minutes

Method:

1. Prepare as for short crust pastry; add the sugar and yolk to the dry ingredients and then bind with a little cold water to make a firm dough.

BISCUIT PASTRY

Ingredients:

4 oz flour	**100 g**	1 cup
pinch of salt		
2 oz butter	**50 g**	¼ cup
2 oz caster sugar	**50 g**	¼ cup
2 egg yolks		
few drops of vanilla essence		

Preparation time: 12 minutes

Method:
1. Sieve flour and salt onto a board or work table, and make a well in the centre.
2. Place the chopped butter in the centre, add sugar, egg yolks and the few drops of vanilla essence.
3. Work flour gradually into paste in the centre of the well by tapping fingers into the wet mixture against the flour; if hand becomes sticky, scrape down with a palette knife.
4. When all the flour is incorporated, smooth by pressing down with the palm of hand, lifting away quickly.
5. Wrap in plastic wrap or kitchen paper and let set in the refrigerator for an hour before using.
6. Fill and bake, following the recipe.

ROUGH PUFF PASTRY
Ingredients:

8 oz flour	**225 g**	2 cups
pinch of salt		
6 oz butter or margarine	**175 g**	¾ cup
2 teaspoons lemon juice		
cold water		

Preparation time: 30–45 minutes

Method:
1. Sieve flour and salt into a bowl.
2. Cut the butter or margarine into cubes the size of walnuts and put in the flour.
3. Add the lemon juice and enough cold water to bind together. Mix gently to a fairly firm dough taking care not to break the fat.
4. Turn onto a floured board or work table, roll the pastry with quick short strokes. Roll into a long strip 15 by 6 inches.
5. Fold the pastry in three by bringing bottom one-third of length of pastry up to cover the middle one-third, and then folding the top one-third down to cover the middle and bottom third. Press edges of pastry lightly with rolling pin. Roll out again, fold and seal pastry and leave covered with plastic wrap for 15 minutes. Repeat this rolling twice; then cover pastry and put into refrigerator.
6. After half an hour remove and roll into the desired shape.
7. Fill and bake, following the recipe.

FLAKY PASTRY
Ingredients:

8 oz flour	**225 g**	2 cups
pinch of salt		
4 oz butter or margarine	**100 g**	½ cup

2 oz lard	**50 g**	¼ cup
2 teaspoons lemon juice		
4–5 tablespoons water		

Preparation time: 30–45 minutes

Method:

1. Sieve flour and salt into a bowl, blend the butter or margarine together.
2. Cut one quarter of the butter or margarine into the flour, mix to a firm dough with the lemon and cold water.
3. Turn onto a floured board and knead. Roll into a strip 15 by 6 inches. Cut one-third of the remaining butter or margarine into small pieces and put this on the top two-thirds of the pastry dough and dust with flour. Fold pastry by bringing bottom one-third of length of pastry up to cover the middle one-third, and folding the top one-third down to cover the middle and the bottom thirds, seal the edges with rolling pin. Cover with plastic wrap and put into the refrigerator for 15 minutes.
4. Turn the pastry so that the sealed ends are toward you. Repeat the rolling process until all the butter or margarine has been incorporated. Cover and leave in the refrigerator for at least 15 minutes before using.
5. Fill and bake, following the recipe.

PUFF PASTRY
Ingredients:

8 oz flour	**225 g**	2 cups
pinch of salt		
8 oz butter	**225 g**	1 cup
¼ pint water approximately	**150 ml**	⅝ cup
a few drops of lemon juice		

Preparation time: 45 minutes

Method:

1. Sieve flour and salt into a bowl.
2. Rub in an ounce of butter, mix to a firm dough with the water and lemon juice.
3. Roll out into a rectangle about half an inch in thickness.
4. Put all the remaining butter as a rectangular block into the centre of half the dough, keeping the dough in one piece.
5. Over this half fold the other half of the dough and seal the edges together with the rolling pin.
6. If there is excess flour, brush it off and wrap pastry in a plastic bag. Chill for 10 minutes in a freezer; then remove.
7. With the sealed ends towards you, roll away from you. Fold in three. Turn the pastry round so that the open edge faces you

136

and roll again. Repeat this process twice more; leave to rest in the refrigerator for 15-20 minutes.

8. Fill and bake, following the recipe.

CHOUX PASTRY

Ingredients:

1½ oz butter or margarine	45 g	2 tbsp.
¼ pint water	150 ml	⅝ cup
2½ oz flour	70 g	⅝ cup
pinch of salt		
2 eggs		

Preparation time: 10-15 minutes

Method:

1. Melt butter or margarine in a saucepan with water, and bring to the boil over a gentle heat.
2. Sieve flour and salt onto a piece of kitchen paper.
3. When the liquid comes to the boil, quickly beat in the sieved flour and salt. Continue beating until smooth, when the paste will fall away from the side of pan.
4. Leave to cool for a few minutes.
5. Add an egg and beat thoroughly.
6. Add the second egg and continue beating until the paste is smooth and shiny.
7. Follow choux pastry baking suggestions given above, under "Suggestions on Pastry Making," and in the individual recipe.

Watchpoint:

With choux pastry it is important to measure out the ingredients accurately.

WEIGHTS AND MEASURES

An important point to remember with regard to solid measures. Irish cooks are generous with their teaspoon and tablespoon measures: these are usually heaped, while the American cook levels off the quantity on the spoon with a knife. So it is important to note that where a recipe specifies a teaspoon of sugar, for example, you should use a rounded teaspoonful, i.e. as much above the spoon as in it, or **two** level teaspoonfuls.

137

Tea and Supper Cakes

BAKING

Irish people often say that you can't beat tea in the country. What they mean is that you can't beat the cakes served with a country tea. We used to spend Saturday afternoon baking for the visitors who arrived for Sunday's afternoon tea. It was served on a dining room table covered with a nice white linen cloth and laden with a variety of cream cakes and other confections.

HINTS ON BAKING

1. Heat the oven 10 minutes prior to using for baking. Set oven control to the setting indicated in the recipe.
2. Position the shelves in the oven as indicated.
3. Carefully prepare the baking tins, with the lining paper tight to the bottom and to the sides and corners. Buttered brown paper may be used instead of greaseproof paper or baking parchment; wax paper may be used on bottom of tins only.
4. Measure out all the ingredients before proceeding to make the cake.
5. Use either butter or margarine in cake making, remember that butter always gives cake a better flavour.
6. Always use plain flour when making an egg sponge.
7. Use white sugar in most cakes. Brown sugar gives a better colour to rich fruitcakes.
8. When a recipe calls for the egg whites to be beaten, use fresh eggs only—not preserved eggs. Always use eggs at room temperature. If they haven't been removed from the refrigerator in time, wash them in hot water and dry.
9. If dried fruit has to be washed, dry thoroughly and put in a warm place before using.
10. Never remove syrup from glazed cherries but roll in a little flour to prevent them sinking in the cake.
11. Liquid is best used at room temperature, not directly from refrigerator.
12. When using the creaming method (beating sugar and fat together) remove the butter or margarine from refrigerator at least ten minutes before using.
13. When a rich or semi-rich fruitcake has been baked, leave it in the baking tin until cold. Remove all other cakes from tins and cool on a wire rack.
14. When making a very rich fruitcake omit baking soda or any other raising agent.

Freezing cakes: Cakes can be baked, wrapped and put into the freezer for two to three months. If they're decorated, freeze first and then wrap, and unwrap before fully defrosting.

PREPARATION OF CAKE TINS

Tin for rich fruitcake:

1. Side-lining is done to prevent burning and to ease removal: cut a strip of brown or greaseproof paper two inches higher than the side of the tin. Allow an inch overlap.
2. Make a one-inch crease where the strip overlaps the lip of the tin. This increase will go all along the length of the strip.
3. With a scissors cut diagonally along the crease at one-inch intervals. Leave paper like that for the moment.
4. Put the bottom of cake tin on a double sheet of greaseproof or kitchen paper (or even waxed paper) and mark around the edge of bottom with a pencil or skewer.
5. Remove cake tin, and cut out the shape from the marked paper.
6. To line the cake tin: reverse the strip of paper in the tin with the cut edge flat and facing inwards around the bottom.
7. Arrange the double sheet of cut paper inside, in the bottom of tin.
8. Finally, grease all the lining paper with melted fat.

NB. This method, using side lining, is necessary only with rich fruitcake.

Loaf or sandwich tin (cake pan) when using creaming method:

1. Brush the sides of tin well with melted butter or margarine and put a sheet of greaseproof or kitchen paper (or waxed paper) on the base.
2. Brush paper well with melted butter or margarine.

Baking sheet or jam roll tin:

1. Line with greaseproof or kitchen paper or baking parchment so that the paper comes a half inch above the lip of tin.
2. Cut into each corner of paper at an angle of forty-five degrees and pull corners together, so that the paper overlaps.
3. Brush the paper well with melted fat.

WHAT WENT WRONG? BAKING WATCHPOINTS
GENERAL

Cakes with a crumbly texture when cut due to:

1. Not enough egg to bind ingredients.
2. Not enough liquid.
3. Overbaking causing drying.
4. Too much yeast.

Taste too dry due to:

1. Too stiff a mixture.
2. Not enough liquid, fat or sugar.
3. Baking at too low a temperature or for too long.
4. Too much raising agent.

Hard crust with uncooked doughy patch in centre due to:
1. Too hot oven.
2. Too quick baking.
3. Too much liquid.

Cracks across the top due to:
1. Too much flour or raising agent.
2. Too hot oven.
3. Cake tin too small.

Baked through but pale due to:
1. Too cool oven.
2. Baking too low in oven.

Collar edge on baked cake due to:
1. Cooking to high in the oven.
2. Too much raising agent.
3. Spreading mixture too care-

fully in the tin: it should be spread roughly, then tapped sharply.

Heavy cake due to:
1. Too much flour, fat or liquid.
2. Baked in too slow an óven.

Burnt outside due to:
1. Oven too hot.
2. Oven too small for size of cake

tin.
3. Baking too high in the oven.

Close damp texture due to:
1. Too much raising agent.

Is the cake sufficiently baked?
1. Look at the edge of the tin: a noticeable shrinkage should have taken place.
2. Rich fruitcake: push a skewer or sewing needle in gently; if it

comes out clean the cake is done.
3. Sponge cake: press top of cake with fingers; if it springs back up it is done.

BASIC CAKE—ALL-IN-ONE METHOD
Hollow top due to:
1. Overbeating
2. Oven too hot.
3. Insufficient cooking.

GINGERBREAD AND BOILED FRUITCAKES
Sinking in the middle due to:
1. Too much raising agent.
2. Too much syrup or treacle.
3. Oven too hot.

FRUITCAKES
Burnt outside due to:
1. Oven too hot.
2. Oven too small for side of cake tin.
3. Baking too high in the oven.
4. Tin being lined with tinfoil, which conducts overmuch heat.

Fruit sinking to the bottom due to:
1. Use of too much baking powder.
2. Use of too much liquid, making

batter too slack to support fruit.

3. Butter or other fat becoming too soft during warm weather.

Excessive dryness due to:
1. Too stiff a mixture.
2. Baking at too low a temperature or for too long.

Big cracks across top of rich fruit cake due to:
1. Tin too small.
2. Oven too hot.
3. Use of a raising agent.
4. Not enough liquid.

BARM BRACK

This brack is traditionally made at Hallowe'en. A ring is wrapped in paper or tinfoil and baked into the mixture. Whoever gets the slice with the ring in it is supposed to be the first to get married. This brack is rich but light and is best eaten fresh with plenty of butter.

Ingredients: Serves: 10

1 lb plain flour	500 g	4 cups
½ oz fresh yeast	15 g	1 tbsp.
(or 1 teaspoon dried yeast)		
1 oz sugar	25 g	1½ tbsp.
3 tablespoons tepid milk		
½ pint milk	275 ml	1¼ cups
2 oz butter or margarine	50 g	¼ cup
2 oz sugar	50 g	¼ cup
1 egg		
12 oz raisins	350 g	2 cups
4 oz mixed peel	100 g	⅔ cups

Preparation time: 20 minutes

Resting time: 1–1½ hours

Cooking time: 40–50 minutes

Oven position: centre

Oven temperature:
gas 6, 200°C, 400°F

Method:
1. Line and grease a deep round tin 9 inches in diameter.
2. Sieve the flour and salt into a bowl and leave in a warm place.
3. Put the yeast, 2 tablespoons sugar and 3 tablespoons of tepid milk into a cup and use a spoon to cream together. Leave in a warm place for about 20 minutes until the surface is frothy.
4. Put the milk and butter or margarine into a saucepan; bring to the boil and allow to cool until tepid.
5. Pour the creamed yeast into the flour with sugar and egg, keeping back a little egg. Mix to a loose dough with the tepid milk, butter or margarine.
6. Knead well on a floured board or work table.

141

7. Shake a little flour into the bowl, return dough to bowl, cover with a damp cloth and leave in a warm place for 40 to 50 minutes until dough has doubled its original size.
8. Turn dough onto a floured work table and knead the fruit gradually into the dough.
9. Put into prepared tin.
10. Cover with a damp cloth and leave to rise for a further 20 minutes in a warm place.
11. Brush the top with egg yolk, put into the oven and bake for 40 to 50 minutes.
12. When baked turn onto a wire rack to cool.

GINGERBREAD

Good gingerbread is quick and easy to prepare, it was always a favourite with children at home because of its sweet nutty flavour and lovely brown colour.

Ingredients: Serves: 10

9 oz flour	250 g	2¼ cups
pinch of salt		
½ teaspoon bread soda		
½ teaspoon mixed spice		
2 teaspoons ground ginger		
4 oz brown sugar	100 g	½ cup
4 oz butter or margarine	100 g	½ cup
4 level tablespoons treacle		
4 level tablespoons golden syrup		
1 egg		
3 tablespoons milk		

Preparation time: 20 minutes
Oven position: centre

Cooking time: 50–55 minutes
Oven temperature:
gas 4, 180°C, 360°F

Method:
1. Line and grease an 8-inch cake tin.
2. Sieve the flour, salt and baking soda into a bowl. Add the spices and sugar. Cut and rub in the butter or margarine.
3. Heat the treacle and syrup in a saucepan. Cool slightly; add the beaten egg and milk and pour contents into the centre of the dry ingredients.
4. Mix well together until smooth.
5. Put into prepared cake tin, set into the oven, and bake for 50 to 55 minutes.
6. Cool on a wire rack.

ALMOND RING

They say this is very similar to what Americans call almond coffee cake or coffee ring—the *piéce de resistance* of a Sunday breakfast westwards across the water. Hard to believe, since it's one of the richest *Irish* inventions.

Ingredients:

dough:

1 lb flour	**500 g**	4 cups
½ oz fresh yeast	**15 g**	1 tbsp.
(or 1 teaspoon dried yeast)		
2–3 tablespoons tepid milk		
2 tablespoon sugar		
½ pint milk	**275 ml**	1¼ cups
2 oz sugar	**50 g**	¼ cup
2 oz margarine	**50 g**	¼ cup
egg yolk		

filling:

2 oz margarine	**50 g**	¼ cup
4 oz raisins	**100 g**	⅔ cup
2 oz chopped cherries	**50 g**	⅓ cup
2 oz sugar	**50 g**	¼ cup
2 oz ground almonds	**50 g**	⅓ cup
2 teaspoons cinnamon		

icing:

8 oz icing sugar	**250 g**	1 cup
2–3 tablespoons water		
2 oz chopped almonds	**50 g**	¼ cup

Preparation time: 25 minutes   **Cooking time:** 25–30 minutes
Proving time: 20 minutes
Oven position: top   **Oven temperature:** gas 6, 200°C, 400°F

Method for dough:

1. Sieve the flour and salt into a bowl and leave in a warm place.
2. Cream the yeast, 2 tablespoons of sugar and 2 or 3 tablespoons tepid milk together; leave in a warm place for approximately 20 minutes until the surface is covered with bubbles.
3. Put milk and margarine into a saucepan, bring to the boil and allow to cool to point where it's tepid.
4. Pour the creamed yeast mixture into the flour, along with sugar and egg yolk; mix to a loose dough with the milk mixture.
5. Knead well on a floured board or worktable.
6. Shake a little flour into bowl; return dough to bowl, cover with damp cloth and leave it in a warm place for 40 to 50 minutes until dough has doubled its original size.

Method for filling:

1. Melt margarine, add raisins,

cherries, sugar, ground almonds and cinnamon.
2. Mix well together and allow to cool.

Method for completing rings:
1. Roll out the dough into a long strip 18 inches by 8 inches.
2. Spread the fruit mix over the dough and roll up. Avoid spreading fruit too close to the edges. Shape into a round ring and set ring on a lightly greased baking sheet.
3. Cover and leave to rest in a warm place for 25 minutes, then put into the oven and bake for 25 to 30 minutes. When baked, place on a wire tray to cool.
4. Sieve the icing sugar into a bowl, add two or three tablespoons boiling water, and mix well together.
5. Pour icing over the ring and sprinkle with chopped almonds.

ROCK BUNS

These are simple confections of dried fruit added to a rich dough, often served with afternoon tea and best when eaten hot.

Ingredients: Serves: 10

8 oz flour	**225 g**	2 cups
pinch of salt		
1 teaspoon baking powder		
½ teaspoon mixed spice		
3 oz butter or margarine	**75 g**	⅓ cup
3 oz brown or caster sugar	**75 g**	⅓ cup
2 oz raisins	**50 g**	⅓ cup
1 oz candied peel	**25 g**	⅙ cup
1 egg		
1–2 tablespoons milk		

Preparation time: 10 minutes   **Cooking time:** 20–25 minutes
Oven position: top   **Oven temperature:** gas 6, 200°C, 400°F

Method:

1. Sieve flour and salt into a bowl; add the baking powder and mixed spice.
2. Rub in the butter or margarine; add the sugar, raisins and fruit.
3. Beat the egg with a little milk; add to dry ingredients and mix to a stiff dough.
4. Divide into 10 portions and arrange in small heaps on a greased baking sheet. Set into the oven and bake for 20 to 25 minutes.
5. Cool on a wire rack.

DOUGHNUTS

An international favourite, doughnuts are quick and easy to prepare and cook and are especially delicious when still warm and sprinkled with sugar.

Ingredients: Serves: 8

8 oz flour	**225 g**	2 cups
pinch of salt		
2 oz butter or margarine	**50 g**	
1 oz caster sugar	**50 g**	1½ tbsp.
1 teaspoon baking powder		
1 egg		
1-2 tablespoons milk		
1-2 tablespoons sugar		
bath of oil		

Preparation time: 12 minutes   Cooking time: 4–6 minutes

Method:

1. Sieve flour and salt into a bowl.
2. Rub in the butter or margarine, add finely granulated sugar and baking powder, mix well together.
3. Beat the egg with a little milk, add to the dry ingredients and mix to a firm dough.
4. Turn onto a floured board; knead and roll out to half-inch thickness. Using a 3-inch cutter or tea cup, cut out the dough; cut out the centre with a small cutter, a half-inch in diameter.
5. Half fill a deep pan with oil and heat to 375°F (test temperature by putting a piece of bread into the hot oil; if it turns brown in one minute the fat is right).
6. Fry in fat till golden brown.
7. Drain doughnuts on kitchen paper and roll them in the sugar.

PORTER CAKE

In 1759 Uncle Arthur Guinness began brewing his porter from brown malt. It was a brown beer. The very dark stout we know today is a porter of a different kind, but is used as the old porter was to moisten and add flavour and zest to fruitcake.

Ingredients:

1 lb flour	**500 g**	4 cups
pinch of salt		
½ teaspoon breadsoda		¼ cup
8 oz caster sugar	**225 g**	1 cup
8 oz butter or margarine	**225 g**	1 cup
pinch of nutmeg		
pinch of mixed spice		
pinch of cinnamon		
1 lb sultanas or raisins	**500 g**	2¾ cups
4 oz mixed peel	**100 g**	⅔ cup
1 large egg		
¼ pint Guinness	**150 ml**	½ cup

Preparation time: 25 minutes

Oven position: centre

Cooking time: 1½ hours

Oven temperature:
gas 4, 180°C, 350°F

Method:

1. Line and grease a deep 9-inch cake tin.
2. Sieve flour, salt and breadsoda into a bowl.
3. Rub in the butter or margarine until the mixture is as fine as breadcrumbs.
4. Add remaining dry ingredients and mix well together.
5. Beat the egg and Guinness together and add to the mixed dry ingredients.
6. Put into prepared tin and bake for 1½ hours.

FOUR-EGG SPONGE

This is a quick and easy way of making an egg sponge, especially suitable if a manual whisk or beater is being used. Egg sponges are popular here because of their simplicity and lightness; they are best eaten when very fresh.

An egg sponge is generally served filled with jam and fresh whipped cream, with icing sugar sieved over the top.

Ingredients: Serves: 6–8

1 tablespoon melted margarine		
4 eggs		
4 oz caster sugar	100 g	½ cup
a few drops of flavouring (vanilla or lemon essence)		
3½ oz plain flour	100 g	1 cup
pinch of salt		

Preparation time: 15 minutes **Cooking time:** 12–15 minutes

Oven position: top **Oven temperature:** gas 6, 200°C, 400°F

Method:

1. Prepare two round cake tins well-greased with melted margarine.
2. Separate egg yolks from whites.
3. Beat the whites until firm (but not dry).
4. Add sugar, yolks and a little flavouring. Beat until thick and creamy.
5. Sieve flour and salt together and fold into the beaten eggs and sugar. Pour into two prepared tins and bake for 12 to 15 minutes.
6. When baked, turn out and cool on a wire rack.

JAM SPONGE ROLL

This is an egg sponge. When prepared it is filled with hot jam, then immediately rolled up and put on a wire rack to cool. It is cut into slices before being served, and is best served fresh.

146

Ingredients: **Serves: 10**

Use same ingredients as for four-egg sponge, plus
3–4 tablespoons heated jam (raspberry or strawberry)

Preparation time: 15 minutes   **Cooking time:** 12–15 minutes
Oven position: centre   **Oven temperature:**
                                     gas 6, 200°C, 400°F

Method:
1. Line and grease a baking sheet.
2. Prepare as for egg sponge.
3. Pour mixture onto a prepared baking sheet, and bake for 12 to 15 minutes.
4. Meantime lay a damp tea towel out flat on a board or work table; lay a sheet of greaseproof paper on top. Sprinkle paper with a little sugar and fold mixture together.
5. When sponge is baked, turn onto the prepared sugar paper and spread with heated jam.
6. Roll up immediately, and leave to cool on a wire rack.

SPONGE FLAN SHELL

This is a very light flan case, generally filled with fresh fruit and whipped jelly, and decorated with fresh cream.

Ingredients:

Use half the ingredients of a four-egg sponge

Method:
1. Grease a 7-inch tin.
2. Pour mixture into flan tin.
3. Bake for 12 to 15 minutes.

COFFEE CAKE

This is not at all like an American coffee cake, which is a ring served hot with the breakfast coffee. This is an egg sponge with coffee in it, and has a nice light brown colour when baked; generally it is filled and decorated with a butter icing.

Ingredients: **Serves: 6–8**

cake:
same ingredients as for a four-egg sponge, plus
1 tablespoon liquid coffee concentrate
    (or 1 tablespoon of instant coffee blended
    with 2 tablespoons hot water)

filling:

2 oz coconut	**50 g**	½ cup
6 oz butter or margarine	**175 g**	¾ cup
6 oz sieved icing sugar	**175 g**	¾ cup
1 tablespoon coffee concentrate		

Preparation time: 30 minutes   Cooking time: 12–15 minutes

Oven position: top   Oven temperature: gas 6, 200°C, 400°F

Method for cake:

1. Make as for four-egg sponge beating in the coffee with eggs and sugar.
2. Beat for 12 to 15 minutes.

Method for filling:

1. Put coconut in a hot oven for 10 to 15 minutes until golden; allow to cool. Add coffee and mix well.
2. Cream fat and icing sugar together.
3. Sandwich cakes together with a little of the butter icing.
4. Butter the sides of cake with half the remaining butter icing, and roll in some golden coconut.
5. Finally butter the top of cake with remaining butter icing and sprinkle with coconut.
6. If desired, set aside some butter icing and decorate cake with roses of butter icing.

BASIC CAKE

What makes this such a popular cake is its uncomplicated preparation, its durability (it can be made and stored for a week or two), and its adaptability as a base for a whole range of cakes that can be made by simply adding various ingredients. On its own, it can be served plain or decorated with a butter icing.

Ingredients: Serves: 10

8 oz plain flour	**225 g**	2 cups
pinch of salt		
6 oz butter or margarine	**175 g**	³⁄₄ cup
6 oz caster sugar	**175 g**	³⁄₄ cup
a few drops of flavouring		
3 eggs		
¹⁄₂ teaspoon baking powder		

Preparation time: 20 minutes   **Cooking time:** 1¹⁄₄–1¹⁄₂ hours

Oven position: centre   **Oven temperature:**
gas 4, 180°C, 350°F

Method:

1. Line and grease a deep 8-inch cake tin.
2. Sieve flour and salt onto a piece of waxed paper.
3. Beat butter or margarine with sugar, beating for 5 to 10 minutes to a fine white cream.
4. Beat in the eggs one at a time.
5. Fold in the sieved flour and baking powder.
6. Put into prepared tin.
7. Place in oven and bake for 1¹⁄₄ to 1¹⁄₂ hours. Remove and place on a wire rack.

Basic cake: All-in-one method:

1. Put all the above ingredients in a bowl and beat until well mixed together.
2. Bake for 1¹⁄₄–1¹⁄₂ hours in prepared tin.

148

MOTHER'S CAKE

When making this cake, instead of using the old-fashioned weights, mother put eggs on the scales. We all knew the basic idea of the recipe from the time we could count: add the same weight of flour as eggs and the same weight of sugar as eggs.

This simple method produces a result not unlike that achieved by using the basic cake mixture. When it is baked and decorated it looks very good; and mother's cake always had a great bite to it.

Ingredients:

cake:
the weight of the eggs in butter or margarine
the weight of the eggs in caster sugar
the weight of the eggs in plain flour
1 teaspoon baking powder
a pinch of salt

1 oz cocoa	25 g	¼ cup

1 dessertspoon water

filling:

2 oz butter or margarine	50 g	¼ cup
4 oz sieved icing sugar	100 g	½ cup

a few drops of flavouring
(vanilla or lemon essence)

icing:

8 oz icing sugar	225 g	1 cup

2-3 tablespoons hot water
2-3 glacé cherries
one strip of angelica

Preparation time: 15 minutes   **Cooking time:** 1¼–1½ hours
Oven position: centre   **Oven temperature:**
    gas 4, 180°C, 360°F

Method for cake:

1. Line and grease two 8-inch cake tins.
2. Sieve flour and salt onto a piece of kitchen paper.
3. Cream the butter or margarine and sugar and beat until white; add eggs one at a time, adding a tablespoon of flour with each egg. Beat well. Fold in the remaining flour.
4. Divide mixture in two. Put half the mixture into a tin.
5. Blend the cocoa with water; fold this into remaining mixture and put into the other tin. Put tins into the oven and bake for 1¼ to 1½ hours.
6. When baked, remove cakes from the tins and set on a wire rack until cool.

Method for filling:

1. Beat the butter or margarine

149

and the icing sugar together; add a few drops of flavouring and continue beating until white and creamy.
2. Sandwich the layers together with butter icing.

Method for icing:

1. Sieve the icing sugar into a bowl; gradually add the hot water and beat until smooth.
2. Pour icing over top of cake. Decorate with cherries and leaves cut in shape of diamonds from angelica strip.

SEED CAKE

As children we were often fascinated by those little dark seeds in cakes an aunt of ours made from home-grown caraway seeds combined with her basic cake mixture. The seeds give a lovely flavour to this cake.

Ingredients: Serves: 10

8 oz flour	225 g	2 cups
pinch of salt		
6 oz margarine	175 g	³⁄₄ cup
6 oz caster sugar	175 g	³⁄₄ cup
½ teaspoon baking powder		
3 eggs		
1 oz caraway seeds	25 g	2 tbsp.

Preparation time: 15 minutes   **Cooking time:** 1¼–1½ hours
Oven position: centre   **Oven temperature:**
gas 4, 180°C, 350°F

Method:

1. Line and grease a deep 8-inch cake tin.
2. Make and bake as for Basic Cake; fold in the caraway seeds with the flour.

CHAPEL WINDOW

This cake gets its name from the lattice effect of combining not only white and brown as in the recipe below, but any two contrasting food colours to vary the presentation and the flavour. The cake as a whole is covered and decorated with almond paste, and during the Christmas season green almond leaves and red berries (both made from the almond paste) can be arranged together across the windows to resemble holly.

Ingredients: Serves: 8–10

cake:

6 oz margarine	175 g	³⁄₄ cup
6 oz sugar	175 g	³⁄₄ cup
12 oz plain flour	340 g	3 cups
3 eggs		
vanilla essence		

150

1 teaspoon baking powder
pinch of salt
2 tablespoons cocoa
1 tablespoon milk
almond paste:

4 oz ground almonds	**100 g**	$\frac{1}{2}$ cup
4 oz icing sugar	**100 g**	$\frac{1}{2}$ cup
4 oz caster sugar	**100 g**	$\frac{1}{2}$ cup

1 egg yolk
1 tablespoon brandy or whiskey
lemon curd or jam
glacé cherries
angelica

Preparation time: 20 minutes
Oven position: centre

Cooking time: 25 minutes
Oven temperature:
gas 6, 200°C, 400°F

Method for making cake:
1. Line and grease two 4-inch by 10-inch loaf tins.
2. Cream margarine and sugar until light and fluffy; then beat in the eggs one at a time.
3. Sieve flour and salt. Add to the creamed mixture with enough milk to make a soft dropping consistency.
4. Divide the mixture in half, adding cocoa to one mixture and vanilla extract to the other, making two cakes, one vanilla and one chocolate. Bake in separate tins in a moderate oven for 25 minutes.
5. When baked, cool on a wire rack. When cool, cut each cake in half lengthwise, making four cake strips, two vanilla and two chocolate.

Method for making almond paste:
1. Put ground almonds into a bowl and sieve in the sugars.
2. Add almond essence, egg yolks and spirits.

3. Mix to a smooth paste, using hands in preference to a wooden spoon.
4. Turn out onto a board or work table dusted with icing or finely granulated sugar, and knead until smooth. Avoid over-kneading as this can cause the paste to become too oily and unmanageable.

Method for assembling cake:
1. Alternate the cake strips one on top of the other, so that there are four strips lengthwise which when stacked together make a checkerboard design on either end. Use lemon curd or jam between the layers to fix them together in one rectangular unit.
2. Coat all the sides with lemon curd or jam, but not the ends.
3. Roll out almond paste on a sugared worktop so that it will cover the two sides and top. Cover everything except the ends with almond paste. (Cover

151

bottom if desired.) Decorate with a crisscross or diamond pattern on the top by drawing a knife lightly over the paste; arrange glacé cherries and angelica as wished.

ORANGE CAKE

This cake, with its lovely sweet flavour of orange, is generally filled with butter icing and topped with a water icing and orange segments.

Ingredients: Serves: 10

cake:

9 oz plain flour	**250 g**	2¼ cups
pinch of salt		
6 oz margarine	**175 g**	¾ cup
6 oz caster sugar	**175 g**	¾ cup
½ teaspoon baking powder		
3 eggs		
rind from orange		
1 tablespoon orange juice		
icing:		
8 oz icing sugar	**225 g**	1 cup
2–3 tablespoons boiling water		
orange segments		

Preparation time: 20 minutes   **Cooking time:** 1–1½ hours
Oven position: centre

Oven temperature: gas 4, 180°C, 350°F

Method for cake:

1. Line and grease a deep 8-inch cake tin.
2. Prepare as for Basic Cake and bake for 1 to 1½hours.

Method for Icing:

1. Sieve icing sugar into a bowl. Add water and beat until smooth. Pour over cake.
2. Decorate with orange segments.

To vary:

For sharper, less sweet flavour, make it a lemon cake by simply substituting lemon rind, lemon juice and lemon segments.

CHERRY CAKE

The secret of this cake is to roll these lovely syrupy cherries in flour. This keeps the cherries evenly distributed and uses the syrup to enhance the cake's flavour.

Ingredients: Serves: 10

9 oz plain flour	**250 g**	2¼ cups
pinch of salt		
6 oz butter or margarine	**175 g**	¾ cup
6 oz caster sugar	**175 g**	¾ cup

½ teaspoon baking powder
3 eggs
1 tablespoon milk
4 oz glacé cherries sliced and tossed
    in a little flour   **115 g**   ⅔ cup

Preparation time: 15 minutes   **Cooking time:** 1¼–1½ hours
Oven position: centre   **Oven temperature:**
                                      gas 4, 180°C, 350°F

Method:
1. Grease and line a deep 8-inch cake tin.
2. Make and bake for 1¼ to 1½ hours as for Basic Cake, adding the 3 eggs with milk; finally add the cherries.

CHOCOLATE MARBLE CAKE

This is very like "Chapel Window". Three different colours are generally used, with the basic cake recipe divided into three, but with the layers arranged one on top of the other and put to bake in the same tin. It can be served plain or, as here, coated with a chocolate icing and garnished with citrus peel or nuts.

Ingredients: **Serves: 10**

cake:
8 oz flour   **225 g**   2 cups
pinch of salt
6 oz butter or margarine   **175 g**   ¾ cup
6 oz caster sugar   **175 g**   ¾ cup
3 eggs
½ teaspoon baking powder
a few drops of vanilla essence
1 dessertspoon cocoa blended
    with 1–2 tablespoons water
red or green colouring
chocolate icing:
8 oz cooking chocolate   **225 g**   8 squares
knob of butter
2 tablespoons milk
thin strips lemon rind

Preparation time: 25 minutes   **Cooking time:** 1¼–1½ hours
Oven position: centre   **Oven temperature:**
                                        gas 4, 180°C, 350°F

Method for cake:
1. Line and grease a deep 8-inch cake tin.
2. Prepare as for Basic Cake omitting cocoa and colouring.
3. Put one-third of the mixture onto a plate and add the

blended cocoa to it; mix well together.

4. Take out half the remaining mixture and put onto a plate; add the green or red colouring to it and mix well together. Leave the remaining one-third plain.

5. Fill the tin alternating the colours, one large spoonful at a time, and bake for 1¼ hours.

6. Allow to cool.

Method for chocolate icing:

1. Melt the chocolate in a bowl over a saucepan of hot water; add the milk and mix well together. Add knob of butter and beat until smooth.

2. Pour the chocolate icing over cake and decorate with lemon strips.

WALNUT LAYER CAKE

This cake uses the basic cake mixture with chopped walnuts added. The decoration and topping of flowing white icing makes temptation irresistible:

Ingredients: Serves: 10

cake:

4 oz margarine	**100 g**	½ cup
8 oz brown sugar	**225 g**	1 cup
2 eggs		
8 oz flour	**225 g**	2 cups
1 teaspoon baking powder		
pinch of salt		
¼ pint milk	**150 ml**	⅝ cup
4 oz finely chopped walnuts	**100 g**	1 cup
frosting:		
2 egg whites		
10 oz sieved icing sugar	**275 g**	1¼ cups
2 tablespoons lemon juice		
filling and decoration:		
2 oz chopped walnuts	**50 g**	½ cup
6 walnuts		

Preparation time: 25 minutes   **Cooking time:** 30–35 minutes
Oven position: centre   **Oven temperature:**
                                                  gas 4, 180°C, 350°F

Method for cake:

1. Line and grease two 7-inch cake tins.

2. Cream the margarine and sugar together for 10 minutes until light and fluffy. Beat the eggs one at a time into the creamed mix. Fold the sieved flour, salt, baking powder, milk and chopped walnuts into the creamed sugar and margarine mix.

3. Divide the mixture between the two prepared tins and bake for 30 to 35 minutes.

154

4. When baked, cool on a wire rack.

Method for frosting:

1. Put egg whites, icing sugar and lemon juice into a bowl and whisk over a pan of gentle simmering water for four to five minutes; remove from the heat and continue whisking for a further two minutes while the frosting cools and stiffens to the consistency of whipped cream.
2. Quickly sandwich the layers of sponge with three or four tablespoons of frosting and sprinkle the chopped walnuts over frosting.
3. Cover top and sides of the cake with remaining frosting and decorate with walnut halves. Store in an airtight tin.

MINCEMEAT CHEESECAKE

This combines pastry and the basic cake mixture together with a filling of dried fruit and a taste both of spirits and almonds. It is a great favourite during the Christmas season.

Ingredients: Serves: 8–10

pastry:

6 oz flour	**175 g**	1½ cups
pinch of salt		
4 oz margarine	**100 g**	½ cup
1 egg yolk		
2–3 tablespoons water		

filling:

3–4 tablespoons mincemeat		½ cup
1–2 tablespoons rum		
4 oz margarine	**100 g**	½ cup
4 oz caster sugar	**100 g**	½ cup
2 eggs		
6 oz self-raising flour	**175 g**	1½ cups
2 oz ground almonds	**50 g**	⅓ cup

Preparation time: 15 minutes
Oven position: centre

Cooking time: 35 minutes
Oven temperature:
gas 6, 200°C, 400°F

Method for pastry:

1. Sieve flour and salt into a bowl.
2. Add margarine and cut into small pieces; rub this into flour with tips of fingers until mixture resembles fine breadcrumbs.
3. Add yolk and water, bind well together.
4. Turn onto a floured board and knead lightly.
5. Roll out pastry and line a 9-inch layer tin. Set aside a little pastry.

Method for filling:

1. Mix the mincemeat and rum together and put in pastry shell.
2. Put margarine, sugar, eggs, flour and almonds into a bowl

and beat for 3 minutes until well creamed together.

3. Arrange mixture on top of mincemeat.
4. Roll out remaining pastry and

cut into long strips nine inches by a half-inch. Decorate top of mixture with pastry strips; put into oven and bake for 30 to 35 minutes.

LIGHT FRUITCAKE

This cake is convenient for a busy housekeeper because when baked it can be stored in an airtight tin and still remain fresh for two weeks. It's not expensive to make and there's great cutting in it.

Ingredients:

8 oz flour	225 g	2 cups
pinch of salt		
6 oz butter or margarine	175 g	¾ cup
6 oz caster sugar	175 g	¾ cup
½ teaspoon baking powder		
3 eggs		
4 oz raisins or sultanas	100 g	⅔ cup
2 oz candied peel	50 g	⅓ cup
2 oz cherries		
(sliced and tossed in a little flour)	50 g	⅓ cup

Preparation time: 25 minutes   **Cooking time:** 1¼–1½ hours
Oven position: centre   **Oven temperature:**
gas 4, 180°C, 350°F

Method:

1. Line and grease a deep 8-inch cake tin.
2. Prepare as for Basic Cake,

adding the prepared fruit, and bake.

APPLE FRUITCAKE

This is fruity and moist and is a much-made cake because apples are always plentiful and because it matures so nicely with age.

Ingredients:

½ pint apple pulp (3–4 apples)	275 ml	1¼ cups
5 oz margarine	150 ml	⅝ cup
6 oz caster sugar	175 g	¾ cup
2 eggs		
8 oz flour	225 g	2 cups
pinch of salt		
1 teaspoon baking powder		
8 oz sultanas	225 g	1⅓ cups
2 oz chopped cherries	50 g	⅓ cup

156

rind of lemon (optional)
$\frac{1}{2}$ teaspoon cinnamon
$\frac{1}{2}$ teaspoon mixed spice

Preparation time: 20 minutes
Oven position: centre

Cooking time: $1\frac{1}{4}$ hours
Oven temperature:
gas 4, 180°C, 350°F

Method:
1. Line and grease a deep 9-inch cake tin.
2. Peel, core and slice the apples, add 1 tablespoon water and stew until tender over a gentle heat; allow to cool and put through a sieve.
3. Beat margarine and sugar together; add eggs one by one and fold in the flour, salt and baking powder.
4. Add remaining ingredients and mix well together; put into lined tin and bake for $1\frac{1}{4}$ hours in the oven.
5. Cool on a wire tray; leave for at least a day before cutting.

CHRISTMAS CAKE KINSELLA

Mother called it old-time Christmas cake, but I never saw its like in any other home. She prepared it on a flat sheet so that it took only about an hour to bake. Today such cakes are baked in deep tins, requiring a longer cooking time.

Mother's Christmas cake had a beautiful aroma when hot and fresh from the oven. Often we would cut off a hot slice from the heel or crust, and spread it thick with creamy country butter.

Ingredients:

12 oz flour	340 g	3 cups
pinch of salt		
7 oz margarine	200 g	1 cup
7 oz caster sugar	200 g	1 cup
$\frac{3}{4}$ teaspoon mixed spice		
$\frac{3}{4}$ teaspoon cinnamon		
4 oz mixed peel	100 g	$\frac{2}{3}$ cup
2 oz glacé cherries	50 g	$\frac{1}{3}$ cup
12 oz raisins	325 g	2 cups
12 oz sultanas	325 g	2 cups
1 teaspoon baking powder		
1 egg		
$\frac{1}{4}$ pint of milk	150 ml	$\frac{5}{8}$ cup

Preparation time: 15 minutes
Oven position: centre

Cooking time: 1 hour
Oven temperature:
gas 4, 180°C, 350°F

Method:

1. Grease a baking sheet.
2. Sieve flour and salt into a bowl.
3. Cut margarine into small pieces and rub into the flour with fingers until very fine.
4. Add sugar, spices, fruit and baking powder to the dry ingredients. Mix well together.
5. Beat the egg and milk together, add to the dry ingredients and mix well. Roll out to one inch in thickness.
6. Put onto the tin and bake for an hour.
7. When baked, cool on a wire tray.

RICH FRUITCAKE

This was commonly made at Christmas, Easter and for birthdays and could keep for months or a year. The fruit was regularly steeped in spirits for hours, usually overnight, swelling the fruit and giving it great flavour. When the cake was baked it was wrapped in foil for a few days and then covered, at least on top, with almond paste; when this was dry, a stiff icing was spread and then the cake was decorated.

Decorating a cake of this kind is an art in itself, an art developed after much patient experimentation.

An eight-inch cake is generally made at Christmas. This recipe is also used in Ireland for wedding cakes. Various sizes are made so that a five-inch layer can be placed on top of the eight-inch layer and the eight-inch layer on top of a twelve-inch bottom layer. Four white pillars are used to hold up each cake. Silver shoes, horseshoes, tiny high-heeled shoes and flowers are used to decorate the cake. The bottom tier is generally eaten at the wedding breakfast. The centre tier is cut into slices and given to neighbours and friends; the top tier is kept until the birth of the first child.

Ingredients: **Serves: 14–16**

1 small tin strawberries		
1 lb raisins	500 g	2⅔ cups
1 lb sultanas	500 g	2⅔ cups
6 oz glacé cherries	175 g	1 cup
6 oz mixed peel	175 g	1 cup
4 oz chopped almonds	100 g	⅔ cup
4 oz chopped dates	100 g	⅔ cup
1 glass Irish whiskey		
pinch of nutmeg		
pinch of mixed spice		
pinch of cinnamon		
8 oz butter	225 g	1 cup
8 oz caster sugar	225 g	1 cup
6 eggs		
12 oz flour	325 g	3 cups

pinch of salt

Preparation time: 30 minutes   **Cooking time:** 5 hours
Oven position: bottom
Oven temperature: (gas 2, 150°C, 300°F)

Method:

1. Line and grease a deep 8-inch cake tin.
2. Strain juice from strawberries and chop them up.
3. Combine all fruit and almonds and soak for a few hours in whiskey.
4. Add spices to the fruit mixture.
5. Cream butter and sugar together until white and creamy.
6. Add in the eggs one by one; a little flour may be added in with each egg. Fold in remaining sieved flour and salt.
7. Put in the soaked fruit mix and turn cake into prepared tin.
8. Put into the oven, cover with a double sheet of greaseproof paper and bake for 5 to 5½ hours.
9. When baked leave in the tin overnight. Remove when cold.

To vary:

Cover with almond paste and royal icing.

POITIN CAKE

Poitín (pronounced pwah-cheen) is an illegal drink distilled from barley and potatoes and commonly made in rural Ireland. It is clear colourless drink like vodka, and, largely because the taxman is absent from the transaction, is far cheaper than any of our other spirits. The price will vary widely depending on demand and on the shrewdness or gullibility of the purchaser. Many of our overseas friends will buy a bottle of it. They'll falsely label it, for instance, as "holy water", put it into their suitcases, and sneak it through customs for an illicit tipple in the privacy of their faraway homes.

A good poitín drinker will pour himself a glass of poitín and swallow off the entire contents at one gulp—a practice that is not recommended to the un-initiated since it can mean a three-day separation of the skull from the contents of the head.

Irish cooks are very thrifty and so use poitín in place of whiskey or brandy. Poitín is often laced into already rich fruitcakes, though it doesn't corrupt the innocent. The fruit is put to steep in poitín overnight and then is fed directly into the dough as well, moistening the cake and giving it a lovely flavour.

Ingredients: Serves: 12

8 oz raisins	225 g	1⅓ cups
8 oz sultanas	225 g	1⅓ cups
2 oz candied peel	50 g	⅓ cup
2 oz sliced glacé cherries	50 g	⅓ cup
1 oz chopped almonds	25 g	2 tbsp.

½ teaspoon mixed spice
½ cup poitín

9 oz flour	**250 g**	2¼ cup
pinch of salt		
6 oz butter or margarine	**175 g**	¾ cup
6 oz caster sugar	**175 g**	¾ cup
1 teaspoon baking powder		
3 eggs		

Preparation time: 25 minutes   **Cooking time:** 3 hours
Oven position: centre   **Oven temperature:**
gas 3, 165°C, 325°F

Method:

1. Steep the fruit, spices and chopped almonds for a few hours in poitín.
2. Line and grease a deep 8-inch tin.
3. Sieve flour and salt together.
4. Cream butter or margarine and sugar together, continue as for basic cake.
5. Add soaked fruit, spices, baking powder and chopped almonds to cake mixture.
6. Put mixture into prepared tin and spread out evenly. Arrange whole almonds on top.
7. Cover with a double sheet of greaseproof or brown paper and bake for three hours.
8. When baking is done, remove cake from oven and leave in tin until cold.

ALMOND PASTE

This is a highly flavoured rich paste used to coat cakes which are rich in fruit. This coating is further enriched by being decorated with toasted whole almonds and glacé green or red cherries.

Ingredients: To cover: an 8-inch cake

10 oz ground almonds	**275 g**	1¼ cups
10 oz icing sugar	**275 g**	1¼ cups
10 oz caster sugar	**275 g**	1¼ cups
a few drops almond essence		
2 egg yolks		
2–3 tablespoons whiskey or rum		
apricot jam (sieved and heated)		

Preparation time: 20–30 minutes

Method for almond paste:

1. Put ground almonds into a bowl and sieve in the sugars.
2. Add almond essence, egg yolks and spirits.
3. Mix to a smooth paste, using hands in preference to a wooden spoon.
4. Turn out onto a board or work

160

table dusted with icing or finely granulated sugar, and knead until smooth. Avoid over-kneading as this can cause the paste to become too oily and unmanageable.

Method for assembling almond paste on fruit cake:

1. Spread the sides of cake with the heated jam.
2. Divide the paste in half, re-serving half for top of cake.
3. For side of cake, divide the remaining paste into two. Roll each piece into a long strip, ensuring that there is sufficient fine granulated or powdered sugar on the worktable to prevent paste from sticking.
4. Roll each strip out to a size and length sufficient to cover two sides of the cake in depth and width. Roll up each strip.
5. Unroll strips, pressing them onto sides of cake; each strip should cover two of the four sides. Make neat joins where strips meet.
6. Coat top of cake with jam.
7. Roll out remaining paste on sugared worktable into shape of cake top. Using two hands transfer it to the top of cake.
8. Using a knife, smooth all the joins.
9. Roll top and sides of cake until smooth with sugared rolling pin.
10. Store cake for a few days before applying royal icing, so that the almond paste will have dried out.

ROYAL ICING
Ingredients: To cover: an 8-inch cake

2 lbs icing sugar   **1 kg**   4 cups
3 egg whites
1 teaspoon glycerine
juice of 1 lemon

Preparation time: 20 minutes

Method:

1. Sieve the icing sugar onto a plate.
2. Put the egg whites into a bowl with glycerine and strained lemon juice. Beat a little with a fork.
3. Add all the icing sugar and beat until smooth for about 15 minutes.
4. Keep icing covered with a damp cloth.
5. Apply icing to cake by putting most of it on top (saving a little for decorating cake); with a palate knife work the icing out to the edge and down the sides.
6. Allow the icing at least two days to dry out; then decorate cake.

Watchpoint:

Omit glycerine if hard icing is required: for example, if using it to coat a wedding cake.

161

Desserts

EVERYDAY SWEET

A kind of soda apple cake, which can use stale bread for an inexpensive dessert.

Ingredients: **Serves: 4–6**

6 slices bread		
2 oz butter or margarine	**50 g**	¼ cup
1 lb cooking apples	**500 g**	4–5 apples
1 teaspoon cinamon		
2 oz sugar	**50 g**	¼ cup
2 eggs		
¾ pint heated milk	**250 ml**	2 cups

Preparation time: 15 minutes   **Cooking time:** 40 minutes
Oven position: centre   **Oven temperature:**
                                                              gas 4, 180°C, 350°F

Method:

1. Butter bread with half the butter and cut into 2-inch squares.
2. Peel, core and slice the apples.
3. Heat remaining butter and soften apples in it.
4. Grease pie dish; arrange a layer of bread in the bottom then a layer of apples; sprinkle with cinammon and sugar.
5. Continue layering apples and bread, finishing with a layer of bread.
6. Beat the eggs and pour the heated milk onto them.
7. Beat eggs and milk well, and pour over bread and apples.
8. Bake in the oven for 40 minutes.
9. Serve hot.

SHORTBREAD PIE

An apple tart often served as dessert pie on Sundays used to be made in a very deep aluminum plate. Today we would make it in a flan sponge tin or flan ring.

Ingredients: **Serves: 6**

9 oz plain flour	**250 g**	2¼ cups
pinch of salt		
6oz butter or margarine	**175 g**	¾ cup
3 oz sugar	**75 g**	⅜ cup
2 egg yolks		
2 large cooking apples		

162

2 oz demerara sugar	**50 g**	¼ cup
2 oz sultanas	**50 g**	⅓ cup
2 rounded tablespoons bramble jelly		
whipped cream or custard sauce		

Preparation time: 20 minutes   **Cooking time:** 35–45 minutes
Oven position: centre   **Oven temperature:**
gas 5, 190°C, 375°F

Method:

1. Sieve flour and salt into a bowl, rub in fat with finger tips until it resembles fine breadcrumbs. Add sugar and egg yolks.
2. Knead the mixture, reserve one-third. Line an 8-inch flan tin or cake tin with the remaining pastry. (If using a flan ring put it on a serving plate.)
3. Peel, core and slice apples, mix with the demerara sugar and raisins. Spread base on shortbread with bramble jelly and cover with apple and raisins.
4. Sprinkle reserved crumb mixture (pastry) over fruit, press down lightly and bake for 55 minutes.
5. Remove flan ring and serve hot or cold, with topping of lightly whipped cream or custard sauce.

DATE AND CHERRY PUDDING

This recipe is popular all year round: in summer months because fresh cherries are available; in the winter months because it is served fresh from the oven with a hot custard sauce

Ingredients: **Serves: 6**

3 oz margarine	**75 g**	⅓ cup
4 oz caster sugar	**100 g**	½ cup
2 eggs		
6 oz flour	**175 g**	1½ cups
pinch of salt		
1 teaspoon baking powder		
2 oz chopped glacé cherries	**50 g**	⅓ cup
2 oz chopped dates	**50 g**	⅓ cup
1 pint custard sauce	**575 ml**	2½ cups

Preparation time: 20 minutes   **Cooking time:** 45 minutes
Oven position: centre   **Oven temperature:**
gas 6, 200°C, 400°F

Method:

1. Grease 6 dariole moulds or 6 custard cups.
2. Cream the margarine and sugar well together. Add eggs one by one.
3. Fold in the sieved flour, salt

163

and baking soda.

4. Mix in the cherries and dates and turn the pudding mixture into prepared moulds or cups.
5. Place moulds in a deep tin half filled with boiling water. Cover the entire tin with tinfoil and bake in the oven for 45 minutes.
6. When baked, turn pudding onto serving plate and serve hot with custard sauce.

Watchpoint:

In Ireland fresh cherries are available during the summer months. They can be bought the whole year round in cans or glazed. Canned cherries are expensive and so are used mainly in gateaux. The less expensive glacé cherries usually used in cakes are preserved in syrup.

Some people find that when they make a cherry cake the cherries sink to the bottom. They try, unfortunately, to wash and dry the cherries to prevent this. But the only thing necessary is to roll the syrupy cherries in flour before adding them to the cake mixture. This will assure that the cherries are evenly distributed through the cake, preserving their full natural richness.

HEART OF IRELAND

I remember when I was a child seeing fine tarts, pies and cakes being baked over an open hearth fire on a big flat baking sheet. They always had a lovely brown crust. For those who have plenty of fruit available this is a splendid modern equivalent.

Ingredients: Serves: 6

6 oz shortcrust pastry		
1 lb fruit (gooseberries, rhubarb, apples)	**500 g**	4 cups
3 oz sugar	**75 g**	½ cup
a little beaten egg or milk		

Preparation time: 30 minutes **Cooking time:** 35–45 minutes
Oven position: top **Oven temperature:** gas 6, 200°C, 400°F

Method:

1. Make pastry and leave covered in the refrigerator.
2. Meantime prepare the fruit.
3. Cut the pastry in two, roll out each piece to cover a 9-inch round plate.
4. Lay one round piece of pastry on plate. Trim the edges of bottom round of pastry.
5. Arrange half the fruit on pastry, sprinkle with sugar, pile remaining fruit on top.
6. Damp the edge of this bottom round of pastry with cold water. Cover with the second round of pastry. Press edges well together.
7. Trim edges and decorate.
8. Brush pastry with beaten egg.

164

Watchpoint:
If using a glass or ceramic plate for   the bottom of the tart.
cooking, set it on a baking sheet to
attract additional heat and brown

GOOSEBERRY AND CUSTARD TART

Irishwomen always had a knack for making pastry. Even if they never weighed the ingredients, they could always make delicious tarts like the ones in this recipe. On farms they use cream or milk in the pastry because it was there in abundance.

Ingredients: Serves: 6

4 oz shortcrust pastry
9 oz gooseberries   **250 g**   2½ cups
½ pint milk   **275 ml**   1¼ cups
1 tablespoon water
2 eggs
1 tablespoon sugar

Preparation time: 2¼ minutes   **Cooking time:** 35 minutes
Oven position: centre   **Oven temperature:**
                                      gas 5, 190°C, 375°F

Method:

1. Make shortcrust pastry. Roll it out and line a 7-inch cake tin with it. Cover with greaseproof paper weighed down with some rice, and bake for 10 minutes.
2. Meantime remove tops and tails from gooseberries, place in a saucepan with water; cook over a moderate heat for 5 minutes. Allow to cool.
3. Bring the milk to boiling point in a saucepan; meantime cream the eggs and sugar together.
4. Pour the heated milk onto the creamed eggs.
5. Put the gooseberries into flan case and pour egg custard over. Place in the oven and bake about 25 to 35 minutes until set.

CROWNED RHUBARB

Rhubarb can be bitter during its season and so sugar is generally added during cooking. To sweeten it still further, it is served with a sponge cake or—for a really dressy presentation—under a meringue as in this recipe.

Ingredients: Serves: 6

6 oz fleur pastry
filling:
4-6 sticks rhubarb
2 oz granulated sugar   **50 g**   ¼ cup
1 tablespoon water

165

2 egg whites
3 oz caster sugar   75 g $\frac{1}{2}$ cup
2 oz almond flakes   50 g $\frac{1}{3}$ cup

Preparation time: 25 minutes   **Cooking time:** 30–35 minutes
Oven position: centre   **Oven temperature:**
(gas 5, 190°C, 375°F)

Method:

1. Make pastry; roll it out and line a 9-inch flan ring set on a plate.
2. Wipe rhubarb with a damp cloth, cut into 1-inch lengths, put into saucepan with granulated sugar and a little water; stew for 10 to 15 minutes over a gentle heat, when it should be a fine pulp; then put through a sieve.
3. Pour rhubarb into pastry shell.
4. Beat egg whites until firm, add half the sugar and continue beating until meringue stands in peaks; then fold in the remaining sugar.
5. Arrange meringue on top of rhubarb.
6. Sprinkle with almonds and set into oven 30 to 35 minutes until meringue is golden.
7. Serve hot or cold.

Watchpoint:
Rhubarb is best at the beginning of the season because it is tender then. No peeling is necessary: just a rub of a damp clean cloth before cutting up. Towards the end of the season when it is inclined to be tough, it is best to peel back the skin and remove the coarse strings before cooking.

FLAN EIREANN

This is a rich creamy pastry flan, filled with fresh egg custard, with almonds added for extra flavour and richness.

Ingredients: Serves: 6

6 oz fleur pastry		
filling:		
$\frac{1}{2}$ oz cornflour	15 g	
3 egg yolks		
$\frac{3}{4}$ pint milk	450 ml	2 cups
1 oz caster sugar	25 g	$1\frac{1}{2}$ tbsp.
3 oz ground almonds	75 g	$\frac{1}{2}$ cup
a few drops vanilla essence		
$\frac{1}{4}$ pint whipped cream	150 ml	$\frac{1}{2}$ cup
1 oz grated almonds	25 g	$\frac{1}{6}$ cup
4–6 glacé cherries		

Preparation time: 25 minutes   **Cooking time:** 25 minutes
Oven position: top   **Oven temperature:** gas 6, 200°C, 400°F

Method:

1. Roll out pastry and line an 8-inch cake tin, line with greaseproof paper and cover with rice. Bake in oven for 25 minutes. Remove rice and paper from pastry when pastry is almost baked; put pastry back into the oven for 5 minutes to dry out.
2. Blend cornflour with egg yolks. Add a little of the cold milk.
3. Put remaining milk into a saucepan and bring to the boil.
4. Pour heated milk onto the egg yolks and cornflour stirring all the time. Rinse saucepan in cold water.
5. Pour the liquid back into saucepan, bring back to boiling point over a gentle heat stirring continuously with a wooden spoon. Add sugar, ground almonds and vanilla essence.
6. Pour into pastry shell. Allow to cool.
7. Decorate with roses of cream, almonds and cherries.

MINCEMEAT FLAN

Mincemeat tarts and pies are a Christmas favourite in Ireland. Most country houses used to have large quantities of mincemeat stored in sealed jars. Our mincemeat combines dried raisins, currants, sultanas, mixed peel, almonds, lemon, apples, suet and spirits: Irish whiskey, brandy or indeed poitín. People who could afford to be extravagant used the mincemeat in tarts; thrifty people made little pies because they used less mincemeat.

Tullamore Dew is perfect as a liqueur for the topping.

Ingredients: Serves: 6

6 oz shortcrust pastry		
filling:		
8 oz mincemeat	**225 g**	1½ cups
1 teaspoon arrowroot		
1–2 tablespoons Tullamore Dew liqueur		
½ pint natural yoghurt	**275 ml**	1¼ cups

Preparation time: 25 minutes   **Cooking time:** 25 minutes
Oven position: top   **Oven temperature:** gas 6, 200°C, 400°F

Method:

1. Make pastry: roll out and line an 8-inch flan tin. Line with greaseproof paper and cover with rice. Bake for 10 minutes. Remove rice and paper.
2. Put the mincemeat and arrowroot into a saucepan and cook gently for one or two minutes.
3. Pour into pastry shell and bake for 25 minutes.
4. Mix liqueur and yoghurt together.
5. Pour over mincemeat.
6. Serve hot or cold, preferably hot.

SUNSHINE TREAT

This recipe is very popular during the summer because fruit is relatively inexpensive then. It is a very rich dessert, combining biscuit pastry with its nice crisp bite and choux pastry for lightness, adding plenty of fresh fruit, and glazing all this with a syrup that adds to its appearance as well as its taste.

Ingredients: Serves: 6

4 oz biscuit pastry		
¼ pint choux pastry		
apricot glaze:		
3 tablespoons apricot jam		
squeeze of lemon		
1 tablespoon water		
flan filling:		
1 tablespoon water		
4 oz green grapes	**100 g**	1 cup
4 oz black grapes	**100 g**	1 cup
4 apricots		
4 oz red cherries	**100 g**	¾ cup
¼ pint whipped cream	**150 ml**	½ cup
syrup:		
4 tablespoons granulated sugar		
4 tablespoons water		

Preparation time: 30 minutes   **Cooking time:** 25–30 minutes
Oven position: centre   **Oven temperature:**
                                     gas 6, 200°C, 400°F

Method for assembling pastries:

1. Make biscuit pastry and roll out to ½-inch thickness and line an 8-inch plate, flake and decorate the edge. Bake in the centre of oven for 25 to 30 minutes. Allow to cool.
2. Make choux pastry and pipe into small buns 1-inch in diameter on a greased baking sheet. Bake on top shelf for 25 to 30 minutes.

Method for apricot glaze:

1. Put apricot jam, water and lemon juice into a saucepan, warm until running; sieve, use warm.

Method for filling shell:

1. Brush the inside of the pastry shell with a little syrup.
2. Prepare fruit, seeding the grapes. Remove skins from apricots and cherries.
3. Arrange the fruit in circle on the pastry shell, starting at the edge of pastry with green grapes, black grapes, apricots and cherries. Brush with apricot glaze.

168

Method for syrup:
1. Put sugar and water into a saucepan, bring to the boil over a gentle heat, boil until syrupy. Brush a little syrup over the edge of pastry shell.
2. Fill the choux buns with whipped cream, arrange around the edge of pastry shell, and brush each choux bun with syrup.

FRUIT SHELLS

This is an ideal way of using fruit. The choux buns can be made in advance and filled fifteen minutes before they're served.

Ingredients: Serves: 8

¼ pint choux pastry		
1 10-oz tin pears	275 g	1¼ cups
1 tablespoon cornflour		
½ block ice cream		2 cups
½ lb icing sugar	225 g	1 cup
1 oz cocoa	25 g	¼ cup
½ oz margarine		1 tbsp.
3 tablespoons hot water		
a few drops of vanilla essence		

Preparation time: 25 minutes   **Cooking time:** 25–30 minutes
Oven position: top   **Oven temperature:** gas 6, 200°C, 400°F

Method:
1. Make choux pastry. Pipe out buns 2 inches in diameter on a greased baking sheet and bake in the oven for 25 to 30 minutes.
2. Meantime strain syrup from pears, blend cornflour with a little of the syrup and heat remaining syrup; add the blended cornflour to heated syrup, stirring continuously. Bring to the boil for a minute, simmer for 2 or 3 minutes. Allow to cool.
3. Cut ice cream into small cubes; chop pears; mix the ice cream, pears and cooled syrup together.
4. Cut buns horizontally and fill with ice cream, pears and syrup.
5. Sieve icing sugar and cocoa into a bowl.
6. Put margarine and water into a saucepan and heat. Add this and the vanilla to the sieved sugar and cocoa and mix well together into icing sauce.
7. Pour sauce over buns and serve within 15 minutes.

STRAWBERRY BASKET

Strawberries are grown extensively in the southeast of Ireland. During the strawberry season there is a big festival held and each year a "Strawberry Queen" is selected.

169

One of the local favourites is strawberry sponge with cream, of which this is a variant.

Ingredients: Serves: 8

four-egg sponge roll
1 lb fresh strawberries   **500 g**   2 cups
½ pint cream   **275 ml**   1¼ cups
long strips of angelica

Preparation time: 20 minutes   **Cooking time:** 12–15 minutes
Oven position: top   **Oven temperature:** gas 6, 200°C, 400°F

Method:

1. Prepare sponge roll, bake for 12 to 15 minutes and allow to cool.
2. Remove stems from strawberries, mash half of them and mix with a little cream.
3. Open out the sponge roll, spread this filling over the opened sponge, taking care not to spread filling too close to the edges; then re-roll.
4. Cut the roll into 1-inch slices and lay flat on a serving dish.
5. Put a spoonful of cream on each slice of roll and arrange remaining strawberries on top.
6. Make the handle of basket with the long strip of angelica.

SHERRY TRIFLE

Sherry trifle is frequently served in Ireland probably because it can be made a day or two in advance. Traditionally it was made like an egg custard, not with custard powder. The traditional trifle recipe is superior to any modern version.

Ingredients: Serves: 8

four-egg sponge roll
2–3 tablespoons heated jam
1 cup good quality sherry
1 pint egg custard   **500 ml**   2½ cups
¼ pint cream   **150 ml**   ½ cup
a long strip of angelica
4–5 cherries

Preparation time: 25 minutes   **Cooking time:** 12–15 minutes
Oven position: top   **Oven temperature:** gas 6, 200°C, 400°F

Method:

1. Make sponge and bake for 12 to 15 minutes. Fill with jam (raspberry, strawberry, black-berry, blackcurrant) and roll up.
2. Slice jam roll and arrange slices neatly in a deep dish.

3. Pour sherry over the slices.
4. Make custard (see under sauces), pour over the roll slices, and let stand for an hour.
5. Form leaves of angelica by cutting out diamond shapes from the strip.
6. Decorate trifle with roses of cream, leaves of angelica and cherries.

LOG OF ALMOND

This is based, like a sherry trifle, on a sponge roll with sherry but is filled with ice cream rather than with jam. The ice cream is flavoured with sherry and juice from the tinned fruit. A delicious dessert—with a high calorie content.

Ingredients: Serves: 8

½ block ice cream	**225 g**	2 cups
four-egg sponge roll		
1 lb can apricots	**500 g**	3 cups
½ cup sherry		
½ pint whipped cream	**275 ml**	1¼ cups
4 oz flaked almonds	**100 g**	⅔ cup

Preparation time: 25 minutes   Cooking time: 12–15 minutes
Oven position: top   Oven temperature: gas 6, 200°C, 400°F

Method:
1. Soften ice cream.
2. Make sponge as for Jam Sponge Roll and bake for 12 to 15 minutes. Roll up immediately; allow to cool and unroll. Moisten with juice from canned apricots and sherry.
3. Spread sponge roll with ice cream and re-roll.
4. Coat the roll with a thin layer of cream taking care not to spread filling too close to the edges.
5. Decorate with apricots and whole almonds.
6. Pipe roses of cream around the log.
7. Refrigerate until about to serve.

CHERRY CHOCOLATE

In Ireland cherries ripen in July. A very good way of serving them is with a sponge sandwich layer cake covered by a rich syrup or sauce like this one.

Ingredients: Serves: 8

sponge:

4 eggs		
4 oz caster sugar	**100 g**	½ cup
3 oz plain flour	**75 g**	¾ cup
pinch of salt		
1 oz cocoa	**25 g**	¼ cup

filling:

1 lb cherries	**500 g**	3 cups
2 oz caster sugar	**50 g**	¼ cup
1 teaspoon cornflour		
1–2 tablespoons kirsch		
½ pint cream	**250 ml**	1¼ cups
caraque:		
2 oz plain chocolate	**50 g**	2 squares

Preparation time: 30 minutes   **Cooking time:** 12–15 minutes
Oven position: top   **Oven temperature:** gas 6, 200°C, 400°F

Method for sponge:

1. Sieve flour, salt and cocoa together. Prepare as for sponge sandwich layers and place in two 7-inch cake tins.

Method for filling:

1. Stone the cherries and place them in a saucepan with the sugar. Cover and simmer until the juice runs freely.
2. Mix cornflour with 1 or 2 tablespoons water, stir into cherries and continue stirring until boiling; cook for one minute, allow to cool, add the kirsch.

Method for chocolate caraque:

1. Melt chocolate in a bowl over a saucepan of hot water.
2. Spread the melted chocolate thinly on a marble or formica top and scrape off in curls.

Method for assembling gateaux:

1. Fill and layer the cake together with the cherry syrup and some cream.
2. Decorate the top of gateaux with rosettes and cream and caraque.

SPONGE CHEESECAKE

Most Irish cheesecakes are made with a biscuit base—a bit heavy in texture for some tastes. A sponge base is a light and sweet complement to the cheese. This is an ideal dinner dessert that can be fixed a day or two in advance.

Ingredients: **Serves: 6–8**

four-egg sponge
filling:

½ oz gelatine	**15 g**	1 tbsp.
3 tablespoons tepid water		
12 oz cottage cheese	**340 g**	1½ cups
2 egg yolks		
2 lemons (grated rind and juice)		
½ pint cream	**250 ml**	1¼ cups
5 oz caster sugar	**150 g**	½ cup

172

| 4 oz cherries | 100 g | ⅔ cup |
| ¼ pint whipped cream | 150 ml | ½ cup |

Preparation time: 30 minutes   **Cooking time:** 12–15 minutes
Oven position: top   **Oven temperature:** gas 6, 200°C, 400°F

Method:

1. Make sponge; divide sponge mixture evenly between two 8-inch cake tins.
2. Cool on a wire tray.
3. Put the gelatine and tepid water into a cup; stir until dissolved for 1 to 2 minutes; leave aside.
4. Sieve cheese. Put egg yolks, lemon rind, cream, sugar and sieved cheese into a bowl. Make up to a half pint (1¼ cups) of liquid with lemon juice and water.
5. Pour the liquid into the cheese mix, add dissolved gelatine, beating it in with a fork.
6. Line the bottom of an 8-inch removable base tin arranging the top side of one sponge down towards the base, pour the cheese mix over.
7. Spread the cherries on top, reserving a few for decoration.
8. Place the other sponge on top.
9. Refrigerate or freeze for a few hours.
10. Turn out of the tin onto a serving plate.
11. Decorate with whipped cream and cherries.

BLACK FOREST

A rich dessert, very popular in Ireland for special occasions. There are many different recipes. This one is for a crisp, light confection containing fruit, spirits and cream.

Ingredients: Serves: 8

cake:

4 oz margarine	100 g	½ cup
8 oz brown sugar	225 g	1 cup
4 oz plain chocolate	100 g	4 squares
2 eggs		
7 oz self-raising flour	200 g	1¾ cups
pinch of salt		
¼ teaspoon ground cinnamon		
¼ pint sour cream	150 ml	⅝ cup
3 tablespoons strong cold black coffee		

pastry base:

4 oz plain flour	100 g	1 cup
pinch of salt		
2 oz icing sugar	50 g	¼ cup

173

2 oz margarine	50 g	¼ cup
1 egg yolk		
a few drops vanilla essence		

topping:

1 pint cream	500 ml	2½ cups
1 lb tin black cherries	500 g	2 cups
4 tablespoons black cherry jam		
3 tablespoons kirsch, cherry brandy or cherry juice		
4 oz grated chocolate	100 g	4 squares

Preparation time: 30 minutes

Oven position: centre

Cooking time (for cake): 1 hour 25 minutes

Oven temperature: gas 4, 180°C, 350°F

Method for cake:

1. Line and grease a deep, round 9-inch tin.
2. Cream margarine and sugar well together. Melt the chocolate by putting it into a bowl and stand in a saucepan of hot water over a gentle heat.
3. Beat melted chocolate into creamed mixture.
4. Add the eggs, one at a time.
5. Sift flour, salt and cinnamon together and fold lightly into mixture with the sour cream and cold coffee. Pour into prepared cake tin and bake for 1 hour and 25 minutes.
6. When baked cool on a wire rack.

Method for pastry base:

1. Mix all the ingredients together in a bowl and bind until the mixture forms a stiff paste.
2. Roll the pastry onto a floured board or worktable until pastry is about the same size as the base of the tin.
3. Lay out on baking sheet and bake for 20 to 25 minutes.

To assemble and decorate the gateau:

1. Split the cake into 3 layers. Whip cream until it holds its shape.
2. Drain the cherries, reserve 8 for decoration and remove the stones from the remainder.
3. Pat pastry on serving plate and spread the pastry with black cherry jam. Soak the cakes with spirit used. Put one layer of cake on top of coated pastry. Spread a layer of cream with half the stoned cherries.
4. Put the second layer of cake on the gateau and add another layer of cream and cherries. Finish with the top cake layer.

To complete gateau:

1. Put some cream into pastry piping bag with a star pipe attached, and reserve this for the decoration; mask the entire cake with the remaining cream and press on the grated choco-

174

late.
2. Decorate the top with piped rosettes of cream and the reserved whole black cherries.

SWEET ALMOND PANCAKE

Traditionally Irish people make a big batter on Shrove Tuesday—Pancake Tuesday it was commonly called. Girl students in secondary schools were usually allowed time off on this day to make the pancakes.

Irish people tend to indulge themselves on Shrove Tuesday in preparation for the forty-day Lenten fast. Through the year pancakes are generally made for the afternoon tea (three o'clock) or high tea or supper at six o'clock.

Ingredients: Serves: 6–8

basic pancake batter
filling:

1½ oz blanched almonds	**50 g**	¼ cup
1 oz caster sugar	**25 g**	1½ tbsp.
3 lemons (grated rind and juice)		
2 medium-sized apples		
½ oz arrowroot	**15 g**	1 tbsp.

Preparation time: 25 minutes   **Cooking time:** 30 minutes

Method:
1. Prepare batter and fry the pancakes. Keep warm.
2. Grind the almonds through a nut mill, then add the sugar and blend together.
3. Grate the lemon. Peel, core and dice the apples.
4. Add lemon rind and almonds to the apple mixture.
5. Cut lemon into two and remove juice, add arrowroot with a little lemon juice, put the remaining juice on to heat; add arrowroot, bring to the boil and simmer for two or three minutes.
6. Pour a little of this sauce into the apple mixture and mix well together. Put remaining sauce into a sauceboat.
7. Spread each pancake with sauce mixture and roll up.
8. Serve hot, and sprinkle with icing sugar just before serving.

HONEY PIE

This is a delightful dessert, with the coarseness of oatmeal complemented by the rich sweetness of honey and the sharp taste of apples.

Ingredients: Serves: 6–8

1 lb oatmeal biscuits	**500 g**	4 cups
2 oz melted margarine	**50 g**	¼ cup
3–4 tablespoons honey		
1 lb cooking apples	**500 g**	4 apples

1–2 tablespoons water		
a pinch of cinnamon		
2 oz sugar	**50 g**	¼ cup
1 oz custard powder	**25 g**	2 tbsp.
¾ pint milk	**500 ml**	2 cups
¼ pint whipped cream	**150 g**	½ cup

Preparation time: 15 minutes   **Cooking time:** 15 minutes

Method:

1. Crush biscuits with a rolling pin.
2. Bind together with the honey and melted margarine. Arrange in the bottom of serving dish.
3. Peel, core and slice apples, put into a saucepan with water and cinnamon. Remove eight slices when softened. Set aside. Continue stewing rest over a gentle heat. Add half the sugar.
4. Arrange the stewed apples over the biscuit base.

5. Blend the custard powder with a little milk; bring the remaining milk to the boil; pour blended custard powder onto the milk.
6. Cook this custard for a few minutes, stirring until thickened; stir in sugar and pour custard over the apples.
7. When custard is cold, pipe roses of cream on top and decorate with the eight apple slices.

MIST BISCUIT

This elegant dessert uses digestive biscuits with liqueur as a crunchy base for the smoothness of ice cream and meringue.

Ingredients: Serves: 6

biscuit base:		
8 oz packet digestive biscuits	**225 g**	2 cups crumbs
2 oz melted margarine	**50 g**	¼ cup
3–4 tablespoons Irish Mist		
meringue:		
2 egg whites		
4 oz caster sugar	**100 g**	½ cup
filling and decoration:		
1 block ice cream	**250 g**	2 cups
4 cherries		
strips of angelica		

Preparation time: 20 minutes   **Cooking time:** 5 minutes
Oven position: centre   **Oven temperature:**
                                                                      gas 6, 200°C, 400°F

Method for crumb crust:

1. Crush digestive biscuits and put in a bowl. Melt margarine and

pour onto the crumbs, adding enough *Irish Mist* to blend.

176

2. Arrange on an oval-shaped serving plate in the shape of a block of ice cream.

Method for meringue:
1. Put egg whites into a bowl and beat until firm.
2. Add half the sugar and continue beating until meringue stands in peaks.
3. Fold in remaining sugar.

Method for assembling dessert:
1. Arrange block of ice cream on crumb base.

2. Pile meringue on top and sides, making sure all the ice cream is covered. (The meringue may be put into a piping bag and piped over the ice cream).
3. Bake in the oven for 5 minutes.
4. Serve immediately garnished with cherries and angelica.

Watchpoint:

Keep the baking time short and the ice cream won't melt: the meringue topping and biscuit crumb base will protect it.

ORCHARD PRIDE

Autumn in Ireland is associated with the harvesting of grain and with trees laden with fruit. Many people have apple, pear, plumb and damson trees in their orchards.
Orchard Pride is based on fresh fruits.

Ingredients: Serves: 6–8

½ pint cold water	**250 ml**	1¼ cups
grated rind and juice of 1 lemon (reserve empty shells)		
4 oz granulated sugar	**100 g**	½ cup
4 oz black grapes	**100 g**	1 cup
4 oz green grapes	**100 g**	1 cup
2 bananas		
1 red apple		
2 pears		
1 orange		
8–10 queen cakes		
honey		
¾ pint milk	**500 ml**	2 cups
1 oz custard powder	**25 g**	¼ cup
1 oz caster sugar	**25 g**	2 tbsp.

Preparation time: 25 minutes   **Cooking time: 20 minutes**

Method:
1. Put water, lemon shells and sugar into a saucepan, bring to the boil over a gentle heat. Remove lemon skins.

2. Cut grapes in half and seed, slice the bananas and toss in lemon juice. Peel, core and slice apple and pears, toss in lemon

juice. Peel and cut orange into cubes, removing seeds.

3. Arrange fruit with grated lemon rind in a serving dish two inches in depth, pour syrup over.

4. Cut queen cakes in two horizontally, spread with honey and sandwich together.

5. Arrange around the edge of fruit dish.

6. Make custard sauce, basic method, and pour over the queen cakes.

Queen cakes

1. Use half the basic cake mix.
2. Put mixture into well-greased tins, and bake for 20 minutes in the top of oven.
3. Cool on wire tray.

CHOCOLATE PEARS

The pears grown in most country gardens really mature in November and December, and are bottled or wrapped in paper and stored in hay. They are lovely and juicy just around Christmastime, and delicious with chocolate sauce.

Ingredients: Serves: 4

4 pears
2 oz cake crumbs   **50 g**   1 cup
2-3 tablespoons sherry
8 oz cooking chocolate   **225 g**   8 squares
a knob of butter
1 tablespoon milk

Preparation time: 15 minutes   **Cooking time:** 25-30 minutes
Oven position: centre   **Oven temperature:**
                                            gas 5, 190°C, 375°F

Method:

1. Leave on stem of pears but wash and core them; skins may be removed.
2. Bind cake crumbs with sherry.
3. Fill centre of each pear with cake crumbs. Put on baking sheet and bake for 25 to 30 minutes.

4. Melt chocolate in a bowl over a saucepan of hot water; add the butter and milk, beat well together.
5. Remove pears from the oven and allow them to cool.
6. Coat with chocolate sauce.

APPLE FLOAT

In October and November the cooking apples blow off the trees and have to be eaten quickly. This light dish is one of the best ways to use them.

Ingredients: Serves: 4

1 lb cooking apples   **500 g**   4-5 apples

grated rind and juice of ½ lemon
2 tablespoons water
2 oz sugar   50 g   ¼ cup
2 egg whites
¼ pint cream   150 ml   ½ cup
a few glacé cherries
angelica leaves

Preparation time: 15 minutes   **Cooking time:** 10 minutes

Method:
1. Peel, core and slice the apples.
2. Put apples, water juice and rind of lemon into a saucepan and stew to a pulp for 10 minutes over a gentle heat.
3. Add sugar; allow to cool; put through a sieve.
4. Beat egg whites until firm.
5. Whip cream, add to sieved apples and gently fold in egg whites.
6. Put into individual glasses.
7. Decorate with cherries and angelica leaves, fashioned by cutting out diamond shapes from the strip.

STRAWBERRY CREAM

This is one of the simplest ways of serving strawberries, which are freshest in Ireland from late June to early August.

Ingredients: Serves: 4

1 lb strawberrie~   **500 g**   3 cups
½ pint milk   **250 ml**   1 cup
½ pint whipped cream   **250 ml**   1 cup
1 oz caster sugar   **25 g**   2 tbsp.

Preparation time: 15 minutes

Method:
1. Wash and remove stems from strawberries.
2. Liquidise or put through a sieve.
3. Add milk, cream and sugar. Mix well together.
4. Serve chilled.

GAELIGE ICE CREAM

Gaelige ice cream (pronounced in the west of Ireland 'gway-lee-guh') is an easily made dessert which is rich, light and not too sweet. Most fruits and nuts may be used, but the liqueur is the ingredient that gives this dessert its spiritual quality.

Ingredients: Serves: 4

3 bananas
3 oz walnuts   **75 g**   ½ cup

179

4–6 tablespoons Irish coffee liqueur
2 oz fine granulated sugar **50 g** ¼ cup
½ pint cream **250 ml** 1 cup
2 egg whites
slices of banana dipped in lemon
  juice for decoration
5–6 walnuts for decoration

Preparation time: 15 minutes

Method:
1. Slice bananas. Grate walnuts.
2. Take bananas, walnuts, sugar, cream and one third ' of the liqueur and mix together.
3. Beat egg whites until firm and fold into the banana mixture.
4. Turn the contents into an ice cream tray and freeze for an hour or two.
5. Arrange scoops of ice cream in glass dishes, decorate with dipped bananas and walnuts. Spoon over the other two-thirds of the liqueur.

WEIGHTS AND MEASURES

An important point to remember with regard to solid measures. Irish cooks are generous with their teaspoon and tablespoon measures: these are usually heaped, while the American cook levels off the quantity on the spoon with a knife. So it is important to note that where a recipe specifies a teaspoon of sugar, for example, you should use a rounded teaspoonful, i.e. as much above the spoon as in it, or **two** level teaspoonfuls.

Glossary

Cookery terms and names, including some expressions which may be unfamiliar to American readers.

ALMOND PASTE: a paste made from ground almonds, sugar and egg yolks, used to coat cakes or moulded into sweets (also called marzipan).

ANGELICA: the candied stems of the aromatic *angelica* plants used for decorating and flavouring sweet dishes.

ARROWROOT: a powdered starch, ground from the root of a tropical plant. When added to sauces or other mixtures it thickens without clouding.

AUBERGINE: EGGPLANT (American); egg-shaped dark purple fruit cooked and eaten as a vegetable.

BACON: HAM, SMOKED HAM, ETC. (American); any cuts from the back and sides of a pig, dried, salted and usually smoked. "Bacon" has a narrower meaning in America: very thin strips of bacon or ham for frying or grilling.

BOUQUET GARNI: a bunch of flavouring herbs and spices, usually parsley, thyme, marjoram, bay leaf, cloves and peppercorns, tied in a piece of muslin, or even wrapped and tied in a small cabbage leaf. This is placed in savoury mixtures while cooking and then removed before serving.

BRAMBLE JELLY: BLACKBERRY JELLY (American)

BREAD SODA: BAKING SODA (American)

CARRAGEEN: an edible red seaweed with thickening properties used to make a beverage, medicine and jelly.

CHIPS: FRENCH FRIES (American)

CORNFLOUR: CORNSTARCH (American); a fine starchy maize flour used for thickening sauces.

COURGETTE: ZUCCHINI (American); a small variety of marrow or squash.

CREAM, DOUBLE: WHIPPING or HEAVY CREAM (American)

CREAM, SINGLE: LIGHT CREAM (American); pouring cream.

CRISPS: POTATO CHIPS (American)

DARIOLE MOULD: a small narrow mould used for making individual sweet or savoury dishes.

181

DIGESTIVE BISCUITS: ₁ round semi-sweet biscuit made from whole-meal flour and similar to GRAHAM CRACKERS (American).

ESSENCES: EXTRACTS (American); essential derivatives of a number of different foodstuffs such as lemon essence (or extract), vanilla essence and so on.

FLAN: PIE or TART (American); an open pastry or sponge shell with a raised edge and filled with a fruit, custard or savoury mixture; a *flan ring* is a metal ring which can be rested on a flat oven-proof plate to support the raised pastry edge while baking the pastry shell; a *flan tin* is a mould into which a sponge mixture can be poured and then baked for a sponge base.

FISH SLICE: SPATULA (American); flat kitchen utensil used with a fry pan for lifting fried eggs, pancakes, etc.

FLOUR, PLAIN: ALL-PURPOSE FLOUR (American)

FLOUR, SELF-RAISING: SELF-RISING FLOUR (American)

FILLET: a strip of boneless meat or fish; to cut or pre-pare meat or fish as fillets.

GAMMON: cured or smoked ham; the term refers especially to the hindquarter cuts of a side of bacon, cooked either as large pieces, or as slices: large rashers.

GARNISH: to decorate or improve the appearance of a dish by adding some small touch such as sprigs of parsley or lemon wedges.

GATEAU: any of many different elaborate and rich cakes.

GIGOT CHOPS: SHOULDER CHOPS (American); cuts taken from the shoulder of lamb or mutton.

GLACEED FRUITS: or GLACÉ FRUIT: crystallized or candied fruits—covered in sugar or syrupy icing (e.g., glacé cherries).

GOLDEN SYRUP: CORN SYRUP or syrup similar to Karo syrup (American): a light golden-coloured treacle.

GLYCERINE: a colourless or pale yellow odourless sweet-tasting syrupy liquid which retains moisture and so is used in confectionery to prevent icings and fondants hardening.

GREASEPROOF PAPER: BAKERS' PARCHMENT (American); a treated thin paper used in lining metal tins for baking as well as for general kitchen use where appropriate; buttered brown paper can be substituted; ordinary waxed paper can be used in lining bottoms (only) of tins.

KNEAD: to work and pull a dough into a uniform mixture: the dough is pressed, stretched and folded repeatedly on a floured surface.

LEEKS: SCALLIONS (American); also called spring onions.

LEMON CURD: a mixture of lemons, eggs, butter and sugar which when cooked has a soft custard-like consistency and is used for fillings.

LIQUIDIZER: BLENDER (American); a kitchen appliance with blades for cutting and puréeing vegetables and other foodstuffs and for blending liquids.

MADEIRA CAKE: POUND CAKE (American)

MARROW: SQUASH (American); any of several oblong squashes that have a hard rind.

MINCE: GROUND BEEF (American); obviously this term means to chop, grind or cut into tiny pieces. But the term "mince" is also commonly used for minced meat. In America minced beef is called GROUND BEEF or simply HAMBURGER.

PAN: BREADLOAF or LOAF OF BREAD (American); "pan" comes from the Spanish *pan* for bread.

PASTRY: BISCUIT PASTRY: a sweet pastry made with sugar and egg often used for fruit flans;
CHOUX PASTRY: a very light, airy pastry made with eggs, and used for eclairs, cream buns and the like;
FLAKY PASTRY: a rich pastry similar to the puff and rough puff pastry but which can be made with margarine or other shortening rather than butter;
ROUGH PUFF PASTRY: a rich flaky pastry made with slightly less butter (or margarine if preferred) and used for pie crusts;
PUFF PASTRY or PUFF PASTE (American): a dough made with butter only and used for making a rich flaky pastry for pies and rich pastries;
SHORTCRUST PASTRY: pastry having a rich, crumbly texture as it is made with a high

	proportion of butter or margarine. It is t quickest and easiest to make.
PEEL, CANDIED:	the skin or rind of citrus fruits treated wi sugar and used for baking and decorating.
PEEL MIXED:	the candied skin or rind of various frui encrusted with sugar or syrup and used making fruit cakes.
PUREE:	a smooth thick pulp of cooked and sieve fruit, vegetables, meat or fish (puréed (creamed potatoes are termed MASHE POTATOES in America).
QUEEN CAKES:	CUP CAKES (American); small tea cak(often served plain or sprinkled with icing sug; or otherwise decorated with icing or frostin;
RASHERS:	BACON (American); thin slices of bacon (ham for frying or grilling.
SALTPETRE:	SALTPETER (American); another name fc potassium nitrate used in preserving food.
SHORTENING:	a term applied to butter, margarine, lard c other fats or oils used in making breads, cak(and pastries (because they make the mixtur 'short', or in other words, light, tender o crisp).
SOUFFLE:	a very light, fluffy dish—full of air—mad with egg yolks and stiffly beaten egg white combined with other ingredients such a cheese, fish or even chopped mushrooms. Th(word comes originally from the Latin *sufflar(* (to blow).
SOYA SAUCE:	SOY SAUCE (American); a salty pungen(dark brown sauce made from fermented soya or soy beans.
SPONGE:	a light porous cake, made of eggs, sugar, flour and flavourings without any shortening.
SPONGE ROLL:	JELLY ROLL (American); a flat rectangle of sponge cake which can be spread with a sweet mixture and rolled up.
SUGAR, CASTER:	GRANULATED SUGAR (American); the regular granulated white sugar sold in America is similar to caster sugar.
SUGAR ICING:	CONFECTIONERS' SUGAR (American); very finely ground sugar used for icings and confections.
SULTANAS:	WHITE SEEDLESS RAISINS (American)

184

SWEETBREADS:	organ meats—either the pancreas (stomach sweetbread) or thymus gland (neck or throat sweetbread).
TREACLE:	MOLASSES (American); thick brown uncrystallized bitter syrup obtained from sugar during refining.
WHOLEMEAL:	WHOLEWHEAT (American); flour made from the entire wheat kernel.

Cook's Notes